CALIFORNIA CAVALIER
The Journal of Captain Thomas Fallon

California Cavalier

The Journal of Captain Thomas Fallon

Edited by
Thomas McEnery

Published by
Inishfallen Enterprises Incorporated

Printed in U.S.A.
by
SMITH MCKAY PRINTING CO.
96 Santa Teresa Street
San Jose, CA 95110

FOR
MDS

Foreword

IT WAS EARLY in the summer of 1978 when the bound journal was first discovered. The workmen failed to realize the significance of the faded, yellow pages, encased in a worn cover as they proceeded to repair the vandalized marble fireplace. While they were chipping away some bricks obstructing their goal, it just seemed to fall from a hidden recess deep in the interior wall. They promptly threw it into a corner and proceeded with the work at hand. Days later the contractor refinishing the floors moved it to the mantel area above the fireplace in the library. It was here that I first encountered the Journal of Captain Thomas Fallon.

Many months had passed since we began the restoration of the old Fallon Home, and it was years since I first heard the name spoken. The structure had been abandoned for decades and although it was built in the 1850's, it had weathered the years rather well. Time and progress had inexplicably left it. untouched. The cellar housed a modest but much-frequented bar and restaurant that catered to a mainly local clientele. Across the street stood the recently restored Peralta Adobe, and the San Pedro Square/Restaurant Row area lay a scant few yards away.

Only the briefest sketches of Captain Fallon and his life were known: his fortunate marriage, his raising of the flag in San Jose during the Mexican War, his service as Mayor, some of his business dealings and two rather obscure divorce proceedings late in his life. It was also known that he abandoned San Jose and transported himself to San Francisco, where as one newspaper put it, he "apparently" died. A rather prosaic ending to a life filled with event.

There were, of course, other glimpses of the man in the annals of the day, and his handsome visage with the strong forehead and striking Van Dyke peered down from the pages of Commodore Sloat's biography. Yet this bare outline did very little to illuminate the man and more than one commentator had detected a noticeable series of lapses and unexplained gaps in his life that seemed odd. Of course it is obvious to note that in the case of any number of historical personages we find closed doors, roads that lead nowhere, and conflicting testimonies. In the case of Thomas Fallon we seem to have something more. Yet there were apparently no ready answers for what I was attributing to the vicissitudes of history.

It had taken us some time to arrange the suitable conditions for a rehabilitation effort on the Fallon Home. First, we obtained the house's placement on the National Register for Historic Places (a crucial step in obtaining Federal Tax benefits), then insured proper conformity with City Codes and preliminary financial details. The later dealing with those guardians of posterity, the banking establishment, would follow. These forseen delays gave me an opportunity to delve into the background of the man whose home was called the "finest in all of San Jose," and who was referred to as "a man of courage and discretion who his men would follow wherever he led." Although I considered myself somewhat knowledgeable about the early history of San Jose, I found the story of Fallon taking me to Sutter's Fort, Donner's Pass, San Francisco, and of course to Santa Cruz and its surrounding hamlets, where Fallon seemed to return again and again.

It was in that burgeoning coastal community that the details of his marriage to Carmel Lodge, heir to a rich portion of the largest Spanish land grant in the area, were first made known to me. Little did I realize that when I stood in the old Mission Plaza on Emmett Street or wound down the road to New Brighton Beach, what a crucial element this remarkable man had played in their development and indeed their very names. I also found myself in a small church off Patrick Street, in Cork, Ireland. All of this recreational research had come to an end some weeks before the workmen had their rendezvous with the good Captain. Thankfully they decided to toss the leather-bound parcel aside instead of into the trash bin, for if they had not, Thomas Fallon would still be just another somewhat interesting pioneer, lost in the pages of several musty books and remembered on a solitary historical marker on the corner of Post and Market Streets in San Jose. Such was not to be.

The full significance of the Journal did not at first occur to me; I perused the initial pages with something akin to boredom, and the day was one of San Jose's hottest in some time. Boredom quickly turned to skepticism, and for a moment the idea of a ruse casually crossed my mind. Yet not even my brother John, who told me more than once that my interest in Fallon was becoming an obsession, would go to such an extent. No doubt this was a relic of another resident of the place, perhaps one of the Italian immigrants who had converted it into a rooming house shortly before the turn of the century. By the fourth page (with the writing definitely not Italian), the smooth flowing sentences and graphic, circular letters grasped and riveted my attention. After an hour I certainly knew the immense value of the document I held in my now dusty hands. By the end of the second hour I surely knew more about Captain Thomas Fallon than anyone else, except perhaps the one who had inserted this Journal in the leather case and planted it in the wall compartment.

At the end of the Journal I found several letters, two documents, two tracts, and a ten-page loose-leaf chronicle, written by Thomas Fallon, and obviously intended as a foreword to his Journal. As nearly as I can determine, the first part of his introduction was written in 1861 (note the reference to the Civil War Battle of Manassas or Bull Run) and the second in 1882 a few years before his last entry. Although a reading of the document will confirm that this was a personal and private Journal, this prologue, combined with the mysterious placement in the fireplace wall, indicates that Captain Fallon intended it to be read by someone, sometime. With the publication of this Journal, I believe we have accomplished that, and Fallon, I am sure, is explained in a way he would have endorsed.

The Journal is in excellent overall condition, the only area of considerable damage was suffered in the left hand column, the area of the dates of each entry, and although the years all are undamaged by water and age, the months and to a greater extent the days are badly damaged in some instances. I have recreated them to the best of my ability and where a guess on the day has been made it was gauged to correspond to the actual happening when the historical chronology was available for cross reference. Most of the letters found relate to the Mexican-American War, and Fallon's capturing of the Pueblo of San Jose; they have been inserted for continuity in the text after the appropriate entry. The remaining letter is one written to his brother-in-law in Santa Cruz, and is included to give a further insight into the character of Thomas Fallon, as well as a general character of most of that species known as "brothers-in-law."

There are two rather long political manifestos, one directed to the San Jose Common Council on the land question, the other a protest to the San Francisco Board of Supervisors; both are included at the appropriate date as further elaboration of his political philosophy.

I have not taken any liberty, nor would I desire to, with the actual text. Only in the years 1866 and 1882, where two considerable digressions take place, was any of the text actually deleted. These two are of not inconsiderable interest, but are lengthy and far too complicated to research at this time. Although critical to Fallon's life story, they are largely extraneous to this Journal and have been summarily removed. At a point in the future they may make excellent history and adventure of their own.

The author was conversant with a number of languages, French and Spanish being the two he occasionally uses. Words and phrases from these languages in his writing are left, and in all but a few cases, it remains as written, for most are readily understandable to the average reader. Nothing else has been touched. No grammatical errors were corrected. (The latter a proof reader's dream and perfect alibi). I have divided the body of the entries into five parts, giving each a title, and feel that these divisions were useful to the configuration of the Journal. Fallon writes with a very fine style; he failed, however to capitalize many words and altogether avoided any punctuation: periods, commas, or apostrophes. All of these were inserted to help the reader and for them I offer a half-hearted apology. The continuity and meaning were much enhanced in my opinion.

The Journal stands essentially as it was written, spanning a period of time consisting of forty-two years, and reaching to both sides of the Rockies and of the Atlantic. As mentioned, the Journal of Captain Thomas Fallon is in his own words and only when deemed absolutely necessary will the Editor attempt to footnote anything. Only when the exclusion of such a note, or the absence of an explanatory narrative paragraph would have taken away from the enjoyment or easy understanding of the Journal and the Age in which it was conceived, have I interrupted the flow of the story with their appearance. For these I ask your indulgence.

The editing of this Journal became a venture with which I am very pleased. It has proven a worthy and timely accompaniment to the restoration of the Fallon Home itself. Without attempting too strained a metaphor, it was in a very true sense the return of both the man and the house to the way they were over a century ago. The Journal itself is an amazing blend of history, travelogue and soliloquy, with a smattering of philosophy, and assorted other disciplines included for good measure. It is by what one creates and what one writes that we best know them. Now once again we have the opportunity to see Captain Fallon in a slightly different pose, to view him not as history or contemporary prejudices would have us do, but as he really was. It is quite an experience and an unforgettable journey.

Thomas McEnery
August 1, 1978
San Jose

Fallon's Introduction

ONE DAY I KNEW that I must set down the events that preceded the first entry on that fateful day at Fort Lancaster. I have avoided it successfully for almost twenty years, but now months have passed since the end of my term of office and the desperate news at Manassas Creek convinces me that the time is here . . . My first memories are of a countryside green and misty, and a village bustling with commerce. These are the thoughts of an eight year old boy, and my native Cork was a happy place as I look back. But I see what I want to. Many were not happy. The spectacle of misery and death was not new to the land, and the famine the year before my birth and the one in 1822 were bad indeed. In severity the failure of potatoes equaled the late Great Famine, of 1845-1846, but the fact that they did not fail in three succeeding years made the disaster manageable. The drop in agricultural prices following the war with Napoleon hurt the country people badly; there were beggars, evictees, and destroyed homes throughout the land. The landlords learned that sheep were better tenants than men, and grazing land a better investment than tillage. Perhaps a few years before we left for Canada, at a townland near Kinsale, I saw the dead piled in a stack near the roadway, like so much wood — it is a vision I carry still.

The decision to emigrate was one not lightly taken by my parents. Late into the evening hours the discussion would range, long after my brother and I went to the loft to sleep. It mainly pitted my mother's natural caution against my father's desire to make a new start, with hope, in Canada. His urgency was deepened by the fact that he felt the cycle of revolt and repression was due to turn again, and he well remembered the stories told by his uncle in the North Cork Militia on their return from Wexford after the last rising, stories of "walking gallows" and pitchcaps to fire a man alive. This was not the land for his two sons and so the decision was finally made. My mother's mind, she later told me, was fixed on an education for us, and in the Ireland of the Penal days, one was more likely to end up in a bog or lonely glen, with the White Boys or Ribbon Men, than in a place of learning. The sensation of packing all you own in one small cart and leaving the only home you know is a very alarming feeling.

As we drove the old Blackrock Road down to the River Lee, I believe I was in a near trance. Cork City was built on a marshy spot on both sides of an island in the river, and it was ancient Desmond's fairest city. So I was always told. To me it was the biggest gathering of people and buildings I had ever seen, and the ship we were to sail on was a true Leviathan to my eyes. At the foot of the lower quay it tugged at its moorings and we carefully were packed aboard and deposited beneath the deck. All I recall after that was the sight of the roofs as we sailed and shortly the old head of Kinsale was briefly in view. It was fitting that I saw it last, for my father had taken me and my brother there some months before to show the spot where the Spanish broke faith with us, and the native aristocracy of old Ireland was suppressed by the English. The Great Earl and Red Hugh of Donegal were overthrown with great carnage. The description had left its mark on my mind and it was the last thing my eyes saw in Holy Ireland.

Many days of water followed.

The progression up the St. Lawrence was a bit of a disappointment after the thrill of first sighting land. We were headed for the new areas of Upper Canada, beyond Montreal, where the lands were free and available for the working. We were settled in London with about twenty other families by 1827. London was founded in that year in the crook in the river where the branches of the Thames meet, an east-facing "U" with the main buildings at its bottom. In those days the forest enclosed the village across the river and on the open side, although by now it has surely been pushed back miles.

By the year of my apprentice,* there were several prominent buildings on Rideout Street. The Court House modeled on Malahide Castle in Ireland was recently finished. Also completed were Mr. Wilson's law office, the Mechanics Institute, the Reverend Cronyn's home, Dalton's soap factory, and the residence of my employer John Jennings, where I spent many hours in his company and with his son, Frank.

Commerce was limited to a few shops on Dundas Street, and the Catholic Church was very modest, as was St. Paul's, its larger Episcopal neighbor. Our home was a quarter mile down Rideout Street and slightly east on the South Branch of the river. We had good land, and although we were in modest straits, my father took great consolation that we were "founders" of this place. We had land, position, an Irish Courthouse, and my brother and I attended regular private school. Father would often tease me about the demons and fairies that lurked in the encircling forest that seemed to separate the town from the outside world.

The population at this time was a little over twelve hundred. Most of the dwellings were made of logs, two and three stories in height. We were happy.

My apprenticeship with Mr. Jennings was rewarding and besides the trade of saddlery, I learned much of business and if his fortune had not failed I might be there yet. Mr. Jennings was a Dublin man, and what he lacked in business sense, he made up in a vast knowledge of Ireland, her history and stories. You might say several events came together that began my long journey — Jennings' setbacks, the revolutionary times, and the death of my father. The last is something that I feel even now, so many years and so many miles removed. The weight of responsibility was borne heavy by him and he simply collapsed one day across from the Courthouse near Mr. Sharp, the Negroe's house. It was queer, for he was to purchase said house and adjoining half acre, including a stove valued at $40, for only $200.

Father had talked over the possibility of leaving London, but lately the tranquil mood at Peter McGregor's Tavern on King Street, had calmed him. He used to say that if McGregor could keep order in his public house, then the King was safe in Upper Canada. News of the Family Compact's concessions were in the air, and even the firebrands were quiet. How long ago it all seems

* 1832

now. Yet things come back. I remember how I sat beneath a large buttonwood and decided to take the money father had put aside and travel to the States. Frank Jennings was to go to Detroit and begin a livery stable and I might go with him. My brother would tend to mother and one day I would return. Return with riches at my side. Father thought the States were the new land to be. I left early in the year. Detroit and then the fine City of Cincinatti with its wide streets lay ahead. I had never seen so many painted houses before. Behind me a rising did commence and many of the boys who fought with the rebels had to flee the country. How poor McGregor must have regretted the loss of business. How very long ago this all was . . . so many adventures away.

Thomas Fallon
July 28th, San Jose

The time has moved on much too quickly. I do not feel the strength to tell all and chronicle the many years that preceded the start of this Journal. Let it suffice to say that after I left Cincinatti, I traveled down a pesky Ohio River to the Mississippi and from there worked my way to Texas. Whether I fought with Sam Houston or not is more for those of recent knowledge than for me to say.* Though I will say that the battle at San Jacinto may have been the most confused important event in the memory of man. The writers can decide it. I will play no further part in their farce. I strayed through most of northern Texas, Colorado, and even into New Mexico on two occasions. The times were difficult, but the men in that day knew life better and valued it dearer than the species to-day. They were what John Jennings used to call "full-livers." It was a type of hedge school, but the learning was not of stories and pretty prose. Life was the main lesson and sometimes death. Xervier gave me my first entry — Thomas Fallon will give me my last.

Thomas Fallon
San Francisco

---

* Apparently this refers to an article in the newspaper, Alta California, where his role in the Texas War of Independence was questioned and his later actions in the raising of the flag at San Jose ridiculed.

Captain Thomas Fallon

I

The Journey

XERVIER WAS nearly turned completely around by the bullet as it tore into his back. He was lifted off the ground and crashed into a chair smashing it into several pieces. As he lay flat staring up at me I felt a strange exhilaration — I was breathing heavily and my heart pounded against my chest. I know it was right to kill him and I had killed before but never at so close a range. The shirt he wore was steaming with powder burns. Two men carried him to the blacksmith's shop. I guess it an odd thing to begin my Journal with his shooting, but after it was done I knew that I had begun a new time in my life — things that should be recorded. Things I could never return from . . .

5TH JULY 1843

The Shoshoni wife of Xervier and the two 'gens libres'* are to go to St. Vrain if possible. I will make arangement for their care. She looked at me in a strange way. Of all the people here she seemed to be the least bothered — she spends most of each day with the mortally wounded Frenchman.

11TH JULY 1843

There is a detachment of the American Army said to be headed this way. Spoke to a man, Oscar Sardy, discharged with three others at St. Vrain. They will be exploring beyond the Rockies and to Fort Hall and even Oregon Territory. I will inquire more when they arrive.

Xervier died today at 3:00 in the afternoon.

* Colloquial, for half-breed children.

13TH JULY 1843   ST. VRAIN'S FORT

Arrived this morning. Woman and two boys with me. Marcellus St. Vrain and Alex Godey here also. Anxious to hear of Xervier's death. Confirm my judgement and inform me that Rufus Sage is telling of the awful "murder." Must settle with the famous Commander of the Santa Fe Expedition.* It is well known to all the character of Xervier and the size of the welts on the Shoshoni woman's back attest to it. I would do it again.

14TH July 1843

Carson arrived with ten mules for the expedition. He and Marcellus and Alex and I talked of many things. Mostly talk centered on the end of the happy days. Beaver is no longer able to support so many of us. Tom Fitzpatrick is guiding the U.S. Army detachment headed west. The Bidwell Party promised him to send letters east telling all their friends of his help getting them over South Pass. Louvar and Carlson are leaving for Texas. The Rocky Mountain Fur Company may not last another year. Even Fort Lupton and St. Vrain are liable to be abandoned — Carson wants to try to open trade with the Mexicans at Taos. It has been a long while since the no trade decree from Mexico City. Would like to bring a peace offering of old Colonel Snively's head.

20TH JULY 1843

It is a very warm day. This is surely a beautiful place. Snow-topped peaks rise to our left on the Continental Divide and south the head of Pike's Mountain is like a north star. The Platte is rough and shimmery. Three years have passed since I first saw it — walls, a long quadrangle fort with its towers and six cannons. I came to hunt and make a fortune. I stay as a paid hand. Mr. St. Vrain is good to work for and has taught me much of the ways of this land. Only I refuse to stand on my head and wiggle my feet to attract buffalo — even his brother thinks that a bit odd. Kit Carson says that the animals are quite willing to be slaughtered after the sight of a world with fools like that in it. I have to agree.

---

* Recruited at Bent's Fort in August, 1842, Sage and a party of 24 left on a foray against the Mexican bastion of Santa Fe under the flag of Texas. The tattered remains crawled back to Bent's Fort later in the year. He participated with Colonel Jacob Snively in another assault later in February of 1843. This was all part of the continued campaigns of military conquest directed by Texas President Sam Houston.

24TH JULY 1843

Much to do the last week. Fitzpatrick came in and with him a young lieutenant of the Topographical Engineers, John Fremont. All dressed in a blue and gold uniform, and a party of about 39. He read to us his instructions "to connect the reconnaissance of 1842, which I had the honor to conduct, with the surveys of Commander Wilkes on the coast of the Pacific Ocean, so as to give a connected survey of the interior of our continent." Carson is the chief hunter. Godey is hired. I am determined to make the trip. Pay is set at .45 cents per day for *voyageurs*. Would go for nothing. Arranged for family of Xervier to travel west with us, home. That last word has a strange sound to me. I know that someday I will find what I want and then I can stop my journey. Oregon has a nice sound. Alex and the others are sure they will be back next Spring. The Walker Party made it in less time than that in 1836. I say nothing. I know these eyes will not see St. Vrain's again. The woman and I may both be going home.

Editor's Note: *These frontier forts in Colorado, St. Vrain, Bent, Lancaster, were the farthest vestige of any semblance of civilization in the western part of the United States. Life here was very sparse indeed. In this milieu grew a particular type of individual, the "mountain man." The legendary Jim Bridger was a partner of St. Vrain and Bent, a contemporary of Fitzpatrick and Carson. Tom Fitzpatrick was known by the Indians as "Broken-Hand" or "White-Hair." The first was the result of a rifle explosion, the second a traumatic experience with hostile Indians that transformed the hair color. Kit Carson has been treated well by history, and often resembles the fictional "Jeremiah Johnson" of recent fame. The lesser known Alex Godey (sometimes Alex Godare) was regarded very highly by his peers and would accompany Fremont on at least two other expeditions. He was young and daring with a flair for the romantic. These were a most special breed of men.*

John Charles Fremont

27TH JULY 1843

Hired at less than a third of the rate of Alex and the other hunter. Carson is getting $60 a month. Many of us going on the trip sat thru the night with Lieutenant Fremont and talked of the expedition. He is only about thirty but he has the bearing and confidence of an older man. His style is that of a teacher but to Mr. Fitzpatrick he asks many questions of the Walker Party in '33-'34 and the Indians west of the Great Divide. His knowledge of Lewis and Clark, Bartleson, Bidwell, Jed Smith and many others is wide. Also he spoke of Senator Benton, his father-in-law, and a man who he says loves this land.* There is an unmistakable quality to Fremont. He, too, is on the road to somewhere. I do not know where.

28TH JULY 1843

The Expedition is to head due West, what the Cheyenne call the land of perpetual snow. We are to look for a central pass thru the Rockies. Fitzpatrick and Carson are against this course. With 12 carts and mules and oxen they would prefer the course to Laramie and then Bridger to Hall. There is said to be no central Colorado Pass. Colonel Bent, St. Vrain's partner, arrived today. Sold several Hall, breech-loading rifled carbines to Fremont.** Also a fine Spanish saddle and a French cart. Bent, St. Vrain and Company is always alert to a sale. Godey also sold two mules and two saddles for $200. Talked of the lack of need of this fort any longer. Hopes to sell to U.S. Army. The days are over when a beaver pelt was worth $8 and Uncle Dick Wotton could go north with 10 wagons and return with $25,000 of furs and robes for the American Fur Co. The Cheyenne, Crow and Arapahoe would gladly trade anything then for calico, liquor and an occasional rifle. Now this mid-point between Laramie and Lupton was becoming a drain. I know my decision to leave is more timely than ever.

---

* Senator Thomas Hart Benton of Missouri, known as the "apostle of westward expansion." As Chairman of Senate Committee on Military Appropriations, he played a crucial role in Fremont's career.
** The Hall Carbine was an exceptional weapon. It was flintlock, but breechloading with ready fixed ball and powder.

5

29th JULY 1843

Final arrangements made. Said goodbye to Marcellus and the others. They know I will return soon. I tell them no different. This is a wildly beautiful place set in a valley 600 yards wide, on the South fork of the Platte, with grassy swarded islands in the Channel. Due West 17 miles are the first snow capped peaks, Long's the highest, and south a hundred is Pike's Peak, a guide to many of us on a journey. The clouds surround it. Indians have used this land as a crossing for years and years — the center of the world, they call it, Crow, Arapahoe, Cheyenne, Sioux and others. Perhaps we should have left it so. At any rate, I leave it tomorrow.

The expedition will travel in two parties — the contingent of 39 men are to proceed in two groups. The lighter, smaller one under Lieutenant Fremont will move up the Cache-a-la-Poudre, and attempt to follow an undeviating beeline to Hall. Fitzpatrick and the rest of us will take the carts and supplies north to Laramie and the South Pass. Xervier's family go with Fremont. The Lieutenant made much ado about her, saying that she was desirous like Naomi of old to return to her people. He repeated it twice. Also Carson and the Lajeunesse brothers travel with us. Godey also. The remnant *voyageurs* and *engages* of the Rocky Mountain and American Fur Companies, Creole and Canadians, a German, Yankees, and the free colored, Jacob Dodson — a strange party indeed. I remember when old Menard said a spider could wade across the Platte and never get its stomach wet. Not this year. It is swollen unusually, yet the snow pack does not look melted. Daily rainstorms for a week. Fremont has left. We cross to the north bank this morning, using canoes and rafts. The cry *a l'avant, enfants des bois* is still ringing in my ears.

30th JULY 1843

Blind Chief of the Cheyenne encountered. Theodore Talbot attempeted to converse to little result. Fitzpatrick reports that a large war party of Cheyenne left a week ago to attack the Snake and Crow tribes and obtain horses. Could signal trouble for our other contingent.

31st JULY 1843

Fitzpatrick scouted, got lost from camp and slept out.

2ND AUGUST 1843

Shot two buffalo. Ungainly creatures. We are about 315 miles from St. Vrain's. The snow is still packed thick even in this part of summer. Men are talking about how the buffalo are thinning out like the beaver — end of era, I think.

Encountered Minnekonjas Sioux. Far different from those Indians of last week, begging for food. There is little pesky or irksome about these men. They resemble the Cheyenne, but are taller and greatly feathered and primped. Splendid feather war dresses head to toe, lances and target shield. 48° at sunrise.

4TH AUGUST 1843

Entered Fort Laramie today. Has changed since my last visit. It is built on an elevated level near river, adobe bricks in quadrangular pattern with bastions to sweep all 4 entrances. The burial platform of the Arapahoe boy is still opposite the west gate. Permanent and perpetual memorial. War party of Arapahoe rode by at dusk.

Celebrated anniversary of Jedediah Smith. For the mourning of a victim to intemperance, we had a strange way of showing it. Man mentioned how he heard Xervier was shot in a frolic. I told him it was an act I took no pleasure in. Probably Sage again.

Discussed the possibilities of using the Sublette Cut. Don't believe Fitzpatrick will try it.

6TH AUGUST 1843

We are skirting the Medicine Bow mountains to our west and will soon join the emigrant road to Ft. Hall and beyond it Oregon. The day is clear and cool. Approaching the Continental Divide.

13TH AUGUST 1843   SOUTH PASS

The watershed of the Americas. From here rivers flow to the Atlantic, the Pacific, and even the Gulf of California. We move away from the rising sun. Are traveling about 20 miles per day.

28TH AUGUST 1843

Ride with Lucien Maxwell and the Chinook boy, Perkins, to Rio Verde and near the Lands of Spain. 42° according to Maxwell whose father owns the large Beaubien-Miranda Tract there. Also proceed to Muddy Creek the next day and pass abandoned fort of Bridger on Black's ford. Learn that Fremont has been here a few days before and left Xervier's family. No sign of them. Go past Smith's fork, the famous Peg-leg Smith, not Jedediah, who cut off his own leg and whittled a stump in the same hour.

Godey told us a story at night before sleep about a book, Montalvo is the writer, called Las Serge de Esplandian, a California island inhabited by black amazons and griffins, ruled by Queen Calafia. Gold and precious stones abound. And they say the Irish are great story tellers. It made for a lively evening. We are on the <u>road</u> to India.

31ST AUGUST 1843

Fremont, Basil Lajeunesse and their party are headed south to the Great Inland Sea. We go to Hall. I must comment again on the absence of buffalo. The Sioux are *demontes* at their failure. Large herds used to cover everything to the Fort Hall meridian, and the Bear and Green River Valleys were full. Antelope also. Even the Lewis fork of the Columbia. They diminished in 1834-35, Fitzpatrick says, but now none are seen west of the Yellowstone River. Between American Fur Co., Rocky Mountain, Hudson Bay, and independents, he thinks 100,000 skins were taken for 8 or 10 years. Many more rotted. It is indeed the end of a day for some.

> Ed.: *The Fremont Expedition was approaching territory long in dispute between the fledgling United States and the British Empire. The tentacles of Empire were represented by the Hudson Bay Company, whose mercantile proclivities had started more than one battle. A year before, much animosity had been generated by the Webster-Ashburton Treaty with Britain, a treaty which Senator Thomas Hart Benton, Fremont's father-in-law, had denounced as "solemn bamboozlement." Although the term "MANIFEST DESTINY" would not be coined by a New York editor for nearly two years, Benton, Fremont, and many others understood its meaning clearly. The next President of the United States, James Polk, would be elected as a "dark horse" on a platform of expansion and jingoism. The motto "Fifty-four forty or Fight" lifted him to the White House where he promptly settled for Forty-nine degrees and reason. The Fremont Expedition carried the hopes, dreams, and illusions of far more people than anyone could imagine.*

19TH SEPTEMBER 1843

After a night clear but with dew we reached the bend in the Snake River where Fort Hall stands. A bastion of the Queen's Hudson Bay Company. It is a long valley, nearly 20 miles and this morning covered with snow. There have been problems with our other body. Fremont and Carson and Basil Lajeunesse became the first men to sail the Great Inland Sea.* Four men led by Francoise Lajeunesse were sent to reach Hall independent of Fremont, became separated, and barely reached the fort alive. There is to be a reckoning. Fremont and the Lajeunesses have loudly argued.

23RD SEPTEMBER 1843

We begin again west. This time we go a bit lighter. Both the Lajeunesse brothers and nine others have been paid and are returning to St. Louis. They are equipped with guns and 12 days provisions until they reach buffalo country. We are all sorry to lose Basil.

27TH SEPTEMBER 1843

Cold. 30°. Fremont again splits the party.

3RD OCTOBER 1843

Lodges of Snake Indians encountered. 208 miles from Hall. Near Three Island Crossing. Killed a snake. It will surely be a wet camp if the Indians are correct in their superstition.

7TH OCTOBER 1843

Reid's River. Named for an Irishman who traveled here with the Astorians in 1813, to Boise River. Massacred by Indians. I hope never to have the singular honor of a place named after me for the same reason.

11TH OCTOBER, 1843

Met two Irish emigrants afoot. Both from Clare. Their horses stolen and they hope to hook up with a train headed to Vancouver. The way this route is being traveled they should have great luck. It is as busy here as London on a market day. Everyone is moving west. To what they are going, I am scarse to say, but they are desperate for speed.

* Actually, the great Salt Lake had been traversed rather extensively seventeen years before when Colonel Ashley's men sailed it with canoes in the 1826 Expedition.

9

15TH OCTOBER 1843

Ice 3/4 inch thick on river, 20°. No further entry for now. Dalles of the Columbia. A beautiful, wild spot. Almost Irish. Thru a narrow gorge shoots rushing water. Whirlpools, foam and spraying waves create a wonderful sight. We are nearly a 1000 miles from the Divide at South Pass. A Judge Burnett* and party of 20 told us that Fremont is a few days beyond us.

21ST NOVEMBER 1843

Have reached Fort Vancouver, and rendezvous with the Lieutenant. It is now agreed that we have concluded our assignment to connect with the Pacific findings of Commander Wilkes. Our expedition is formally ended. A decision is to be taken soon. Fitzpatrick, Fremont and Carson confer late into the night. Alex Godey told me another tale, this one of a river Buenaventura that flows from the Rockies to the sea. He says that Fremont will now search until he finds it even if we have to go to India.

27TH NOVEMBER 1843

We leave traveling south in the central Valley of the Deschutes. Klamath Lake is our destination. Now we are only 25.

3RD DECEMBER 1843

Fremont and three others go ahead with the howitzer. I am sorry I was unable to see them hunting buffalo with the little cannon. It is no doubt cruel but very amusing. On our right we can see several tall, snowy knobs. The pine forests are very thick.

10TH DECEMBER 1843

Approach a large misty lake or river.** Activity on the far bank prompts Fremont to discharge cannon at a group of Indians. It was near here that Jed Smith was attacked and lost 15 men some years back. The Lieutenant wishes the natives to know our power. Zindel learned well in the Prussian army and the ball landed close at hand to the largest group. He says it is better sport than shooting at the buffalo. In shooting at a man I find little amusing.

* The traveler Peter Burnett (1807-1895) was later Governor of California, and a figure with whom Fallon will clash later in San Jose.
** Probably Klamath Marsh, 30 miles north of Klamath Lake in the present National Forest and Wildlife Refuge. From here they turn east.

Fort Laramie as it appeared when the expedition reached it in the summer of 1843.

Pyramid Lake, Nevada, sketched in the winter of 1844.

11

25TH DECEMBER   CHRISTMAS DAY 1843

We turned sharply east and entered an area of forest stream, with snow covered mountains on our right and dark mountains to the left. It becomes increasingly desolate. The fog is very dense. Many of the mules have cuts deep into their hoof. Men are very gloomy. My last Christmas in Ireland father gave me a small cross. In Upper Canada, John Jennings gave me an old shotgun. How customs differ. For perhaps the first time in our long journey I feel something akin to fear.

28TH DECEMBER 1843

We are certain to be now in the Territory of Mexico. Fremont now talks openly of Mary's Lake with its rich meadows and the Buenaventura that flows gently into Spanish California. I know not whether he is convincing himself or us. I do not think the others understand him much. Is he searching for a river — or a dream?

1ST JANUARY 1844

New Year. The land east of the Sierra Range is becoming more arid and desolate. Supplies are low. Those ridges on the left seem to darken more. It is easy to note why this Great Basin, this American Desert is avoided. If only we had.

We passed a hot spring, measured at 206°. Now a long lake perhaps 25 miles long and 11 wide greets us. Land is a bit fresher. No Mary's Lake, but we ate the fish gluttonously, 2 to 4 feet long, that Perkins caught. This is to be called Salmon-Trout River, and the Lieutenant has marked it down as such. There is a large triangular rock formation in its center.* It should be called Salvation for it has surely been that to us.

15TH JANUARY 1844

Fatigue is again with us. Hunger also. How far south we have to go no one knows. Even Fitzpatrick is showing little resolve. The cold this night is too much to sleep with. Carson and Fitzpatrick spent most of the night until dawn with Fremont.

---

* Pyramid Lake, undoubtedly.

18TH JANUARY 1844

The decision to turn west was made on this crisp morning with the wind howling about our heads. Lieutenant Fremont called us together and spoke in his usual tones of the things we had shared. Then Carson spoke of the California he had known 15 years before — the fertile valleys and lush orchards. We are all shaken and depressed, but it can't be too much worse. We turned our eyes toward the snow covered mountains. They lay between us and our future — or our death.

29TH JANUARY 1844

Today we abandoned the cannon. It is great effort to record these events. My hands ache and must be rubbed often to maintain feeling. Exhausted but can't sleep.

6TH FEBRUARY 1844

Went with Fremont, Fitzpatrick and Dodson ahead with snowshoes. From a peak we could see perhaps 100 miles. We are a strange sight with black hankerchiefs around our eyes. One man was very nearly blind yesterday.

13TH FEBRUARY 1844

Alex killed the last dog yesterday, scorched off the hair and washed it with soap and snow. A feast of pea soup, mule and dog. I reached a vantage point early this morning and saw a lake perhaps 15 miles in length with no outlet.* A mist covered it. When Fremont and Preuss came up he said that this mountain lake was as clear and beautiful as a vision of paradise. Fitzpatrick had never heard of its location, nor Carson. Godey teases me that they will call it Lake Fallon. I am not dead yet. The snow is 20 foot deep and the men trod on with talk. These passes must be within a few thousand feet of Long's Peak in height. No one would attempt its crossing. Carson spends a long time carving on a tree today. I hope it is not for a headstone.

26TH FEBRUARY 1844

It is possible to see a large snowless valley ahead. The cold is still biting. Today Fitzpatrick had to build a fire in an old cedar to dry my feet before we returned from a hunt.

* Lake Tahoe.

13

Near present-day Carson Pass in the Sierra Nevada. On the right is Red Lake Peak from which Fremont and Fallon sighted Lake Tahoe.

John Sutter

1st MARCH 1844

We leave the snow behind. I swear that I can hear birds singing. I can't see them, but just to know that they exist on the same land is enough.

3rd MARCH 1844

We swam in an ice cold spring today. Derosier is deranged, his hallucinations force us to tie him for long periods. Fremont and two others travel ahead.

4th MARCH 1844

Our motley band reaches the Fort of Sutter on Rio de los Americanos. We have 33 animals left of 67 that began the mountain trek. This proclaimed Lord of the Marshes of California approached us, broad-brimmed hat, bushy mustache and sideburns. I knew he was a rare breed. Behind him stretched a large, low, powerful looking structure of white washed adobe perhaps 300 x 160, 18 feet in height. The meadows are golden with flowers. He said we had been on his land for two days. This was indeed a Lord and once in this beautiful world I knew I would not be traveling on with my comrades ever again.

Sutter's Fort about four years after the expedition

I I

The Land

IT IS A land as rich and beautiful as any I have seen. Don Johann Sutter, the one of the twinkling blue eyes, has been very kind to me. I am once again, as in the early days with Jennings in London, a student. The topic is much to my liking. I wish to know all of this land, this Alta California province.

It reaches from the Oregon line to the deserts of northern Mexico over a thousand miles, and from these Sierra mountains to the sea. There are three civilized settlements, San Jose and Branciforte pueblo south-west of here and Los Angeles in the far south. Missions catered for by the priests stretch from San Diego in the south to the distant reaches of the Great Bay. Most of these have been appropriated by the Central government years past. Presidios also ring the province at Yerba Buena, the capital at Monterey and elsewhere. The population is perhaps 15,000 and it has doubled since 1822.

A war of independence was fought in 1821 to shake the rule of Spain. Since then there have been innumerable revolts and risings on a constant scale. At times the north against the south. Monterey versus Los Angeles, Los Angeles versus the north, Central government versus the whole province, family against family, and the like. There are few casualities in most.

The lands of Sutter stretched 11 leagues, nearly 60 miles and took in most of the Sacramento and American Valleys. He was supreme in this land, a naturalized citizen, and the Captain General guarding this wild frontier. Commander of the Fortress of New Helvitia. He had arrived overland from Switzerland to Fort Vancouver and then to the Island of Hawaii and by ship back to California. His kingdom, for such it is, is based on the labor of thousands of Indians who live in *rancherias,* similar to those I have seen in East Texas. He has his own

17

army, and with the Governor, he is cordial. The former Russian fort of Ross on the coast is also owned by him. There are Americans and English here also, for Sutter has always been friendly to the immigrants, risking the displeasure of his sponsors. Prosperity is the rule. It is based on the trade for hides with England and America. They are worth $2 and $2 more for the tallow. All the Californians I have seen seem rich indeed. Bidwell of the 1841 party works for Sutter. Gilroy of San Jose is another foreigner of great wealth. Grants of land are not impossible to receive, many have been given in the last five years, although most of the richest are already taken. Sutter thinks the unsettled state of affairs will prompt the Governor to sign many more in the coming months.* All land is given only for the use of the grantee and his heirs, that is how all of the Missions were appropriated back to the Government and then sold. Ranchos of normal size are usually a *ligua quadrada or sitio*. Sutter has one of the largest and his *droit de seigneur* is supreme.

8TH MARCH 1844

Rode to the confluence of the Butte Creek.

14TH MARCH 1844

I have been formally discharged from the expedition on this day. Godey and Fitzpatrick argued for a short while on my decision then quickly relented. I now have been given $129.35 to begin my fortune.**
Also discharged was Joseph Verrot, Philibert Cortot and Oliver Beaulieu. The last two men left in a great exitement for they were accused by Fremont of stealing sugar. Their pay was docked for forty pounds at .50 per pound — heavy payment for a sweet tooth.

21ST MARCH 1844

After obtaining a passport from Sutter, and purchasing $3000.00 in mules, horses, sundries, and a fine Spanish saddle, the expedition left heading south down the Valley of the San Joaquin.

* In 1846 there were perhaps 1000-1300 foreigners in the Bay Area. A few were given *empresario* grants like Sutter. Only 25 ranchos were awarded in the Spanish Period, over 450 were awarded in the next quarter century, many as Sutter alluded to, by the last governor, and in great haste. This haste resulted in landmark legal tests for decades.

**For services as *voyageur* from St. Vrain to New Helvetia, California at $0.45 per diem for 123 days, 24 July to 24 November 1843, and at $0.66⅔ per diem for *111* days, 25 November 1843 to 14 March 1844. Taken from "Abstract of Disbursements on Account of Military and Geographical Surveys West of the Mississippi for the Quarter Ending 31 March 1844," J. C. Fremont commanding.

27TH MARCH 1844

A Mexican officer arrived this morning with 25 dragoons. He wore a tight blue jacket and a bright serape with a red sash. While he spoke to Captain Sutter he eyed me warily, and I could tell that he was looking for American freebooters as he put it. After a short talk and provision, this company rode off south.

Have given up attempt to settle on Chico Creek. Ed Farwell and I are not the right pair for a partnership. Sutter advises that I travel to the Valley of San Jose.

2ND SEPTEMBER 1844

Things are slow at New Helvitia. A letter awaited me from Godey on my return to the Fort. After many more experiences the Expedition returned to Bent's Fort by the old Spanish Trail. There were several scraps with the Mexicans in California and they were forced to kill several Indians. He related how Carson and he shot and scalped two of the leaders of a band of horsethiefs. Fremont is in Washington and has sent word that Daniel Webster invited him to come to dinner and talk of California. Alex is to wait for the start of another foray west. This one will be with many more men.

3RD MARCH 1845

Sutter was this year alined with Governor Micheltorena against a group of southern insurgents, headed by Alvarado and Castro with American *rifleros*. An alliance that nearly cost him dearly. When he had marched his native conscripts to aid the Governor and lined up ready for battle, at Cahuenga above Los Angeles, a deal was struck, and a surrender made which left him alone and in prison. It will be a stroke of luck if he can maintain his vast kingdom. His trust was placed in a very foolish cause.

3RD AUGUST 1845   VALLEY OF SAN JOSE

It is a very pleasant valley. The first explorers called it *Llano de los Robles* and there are oaks everywhere. There is a small church, a large square, a jail and many orchards and gardens. I am told by an Englishman that no part of Mexico can show so large a share of bright eyes, fine teeth, fair proportions, and beautiful complexions. Every Sunday the people of the pueblo begin a trek up the Alameda with its fine rows of shaded willows to the Mission at Santa Clara. The dons of the noblest of Spanish families are very aloof and scarcely look my way. I have been here nearly a month and only with old Don

19

Luis Peralta am I made to feel comfortable. The old don traveled with DeAnza's party as a young boy seventy years before. He has a large ranch north of here but prefers the simple pueblo life. Years before he had been *commissionado* of this place and *alcalde* in Branciforte. He is now a *regidores* or councilor who with the *alcalde* rules the pueblo. Many here know of my travels with Fremont and ask many questions. The fear of American emigrations is very real to them.

25TH SEPTEMBER 1845

Have been working at Johnson's ranch in the Bear Valley for half a year. While making a *fausta* at Johnson's I spotted a flash of light on the rim of the mountains. A half day later a band of emigrants entered the valley in good order. Their presence so startled me that I asked in God's name where they had dropped from. This amuses us all.

26TH SEPTEMBER 1845

Have decided to forego these eastern reaches and travel again to the lower valleys, perhaps as far as Los Angeles.

4TH OCTOBER 1845   SANTA CRUZ MISSION

Have arrived here this morning from San Jose. A place that appears much removed from the California I have so far seen. The mission sits on a bluff looking down on the San Lorenzo River and its lines of rich, green trees. Behind us runs the pueblo road to the east and west. The canyon of the San Lorenzo is covered with beautiful wild flowers and herbs. Beyond it is the settlement of Branciforte. This morning there was no fog and the sparkling waters looked exceedingly fresh. A semi-circle of mountains sealed the entire area off from the hinterland north to San Jose. These slopes are covered with the mighty *palo colorado*.*

At sunset with fogs beginning to cover Loma Prieta at my back, I rode down the gentle slope from the Mission, through the marshy bottomland and on to the beach. The sand is fine. On either side rocky headlands push into the water. Sunset on the Pacific Ocean is

---

* Sequoia Sempervirens, or California Redwood.

20

as I wanted it to be. This city of the Holy Cross is a place where one could be content.*

30TH OCTOBER 1845

I have made a number of friends here. Business shows prospects of being good. A yearly census was conducted this week and it has the Americans alarmed. In 1840 an effort was made to rid the country of *extrangeros,* and nearly sixty were seized and sent to San Blas by ship, among them Cooper, Neale and Graham of this locale. Majors and Isaac Graham are fearful of some repetition. The census is only a way to learn our whereabouts and numbers, they believe. It has the possibility of truth, but I do not feel the Mexicans are confident enough to attempt it again. I registered.**

My new home is a windowless adobe of sun-dried brick. It is close upon the mission plaza almost touching the old adobe wall by the orchard. Several dogs were tearing apart a deer carcass on my return tonight.

The Governor, Pio Pico, is looking to sell the mission orchard. No takers. I would like to bid on this property but have not the confidence in my store as yet. I must content myself with the small *milpas* I have for vegetables. If Pico could only wait a few months, but at the speed he is dispossessing of the former mission lands, there will be none left. There will neither be one of his cousins or friends without one either.

Ed.: *Pico's short regency in 1845-1846 was one of unusual turmoil even for California. The capital was moved to Los Angeles, his home, while the Treasury remained in Monterey under the thumb of his rival, General Jose Castro. This resulted in his administration being perennially penniless and permanently powerless. To secure financing he gave away for patronage, sold or leased the remaining 10 of the 21 Franciscan missions*

---

* Another visitor a few years before, the Frenchman Laplace, noted the dirty and dusty condition of the spot, with sinister friars skulking about. At this same period Colonel James Clymons was to note the half-cultivated gardens, tended by Indians in a state of slavery. Beauty was clearly, then as now, in the eye of the beholder. The vantage point Fallon enjoyed that day was probably at the end of Neary Lagoon, near present-day Cowell Beach.

**According to statute the *padron* of 1845 for the pueblo of Branciforte was taken for the Central Government. It shows a total of 470 souls: 120 of these are Indians and 350 are "*gente de razon,*" or civilized people. Of the last group eighty are listed as foreigners. Thomas Fallon was listed as an American, single, age 26 years. Most of the foreigners had arrived in the last four years.

*in the Province; the other eleven had been disposed of in the Seculariza-
tion begun in 1834. Pico also attempted to sell California to Great
Britain, a notable reversal of President Monroe's Doctrine. In the lame
duck stage of his governorship, throughout the summer of 1846, with
American arms everywhere triumphant, he granted large tracts of land
to "worthy" people. This guaranteed a decade of disruption to normal
land titles in the new state.*

1st DECEMBER 1845

New rules are promulgated for settlement. The *alcalde* seems a
good man. The last was removed for drunkeness. Once again a man
may not leave Church after Mass has begun. This was met by much
remorse. Also a permit must be obtained at least a week in advance
for any dance in a private home. The *fandango* is something the Californios dearly love.

A small schooner plying the coast trade stopped today and the
crew carried much news of the States.

10th DECEMBER 1845

I have been asked to Christmas Dinner by Michael Lodge, an
Irishman who comes from Dublin. His wife is one of the famous Cas-
tros, an old family with tens of thousands of acres in the region of
Soquel and Aptos. It is a great honor and a sign of my acceptance.
William Blackburn spends great lengths in telling me how to behave
with the five young Lodge girls. That problem is not one I intend to
concern my thoughts upon.

15th DECEMBER 1845

Lunched today with the Bennett brothers and Majors. They all
speak of the Lodges of Rancho Soquel.* Originally Dona Martina
Lodge had been married to a man named Cota who died suddenly. In
uncustomary haste she married the Irish sailor Michael Lodge in 1831
and built an adobe home on the little rise overlooking the gully on
one side and the Soquel Creek on the other. With a good house she
applied to the Governor, Figueroa, for a grant and shortly received it.
Her brother is grantee of the Aptos Rancho due east. Most of the land
between the two cliffs and down to the beach and river mouth are hers.

---

* An Indian name, derivation uncertain, but possibly meaning "place of the willows." It is
variously spelled Shoquel, Soquel, Osacales, Soucale, Socale. The latter two are the Fallon
version, but for purposes of ready understanding I will use the modern version of SOQUEL.

Just last year Governor Micheltorena granted an additional parcel of land that gathers in the whole watershed and up to Loma Prieta.

> Ed.: *The basis for this land grant was the claim of Martina Castro's father, Joaquin, who received the Rancho San Andres. Rancho Aptos was the home of Rafael Castro, Martina's brother, and bordered Soquel on the east. Martina was a very aggressive and dominating woman. The original grant was applied for in November of 1833 and Governor Figueroa approved it as Rancho Soquel on 17 May, 1834. It spanned 3 miles by ½ league and was perhaps 1668 acres. The second grant which solidified the Lodge hold on the vast reaches of wood and water to the county line and beyond into Santa Clara County was patented by Governor Micheltorena in January of 1844; this was the Soquel Augmentacion or Upper Rancho and was 32,702 acres. Both were patented by the U.S. Land Commission in March of 1860.*

20TH DECEMBER 1845

I may go into a business venture with Joseph Majors. He is willing to advance certain money for the construction of a hotel on the mission plaza. Majors is married to a Castro relative, Marie de los Angeles, and owns the Zayante Rancho. I think he can be a great aid to me in settling my fortune.

25TH DECEMBER 1845   CHRISTMAS DAY

With great nervousness I set out to begin the ride down the Monterey road to Rancho Soquel. It is mid-afternoon when I arrive. The adobe is large, perhaps fifty feet long and commands a good view of the road, the river and a narrow dry arroyo that runs to the beach. The large middle room has board floors and a large fireplace. It is gayly decorated for the festival. There are many guests, mostly old Spanish families. The two middle daughters, Carmel and Antonia, are as beautiful as anything I have seen. Many military men are there, including a paunchy little man called Juan Prado Mesa, Commander of the Presidio of San Francisco and a Commandante de la Guerra. Mesa glares at me viciously and smiles at the young women. I do not turn my back on him.

Today I learned a good deal of local custom and local gossip, perhaps it will one day be history. That tall commandante spoke to Lodge of the average colonist in Branciforte. I remember his words and record them lest I forget their poetic flavor: "To take a charitable view of the subject, their absence for a couple of centuries at a distance of a million leagues, could prove most beneficial to the province and redoubt to the service of the God and King." These words were hard

23

to forget and sum up a view of why the Province of Alta California was so troubled.

Others spoke with scorn and derision of the raid by French privateers in 1818 on Monterey and how in their haste to save the Santa Cruz valuables, the people sacked the Mission themselves. A clever piece of reasoning.

Also the murder of Padre Quintana was again brought up, a favorite parcel of gossip because of the savage mutilations on the body.

It was later when Lodge invited me to ride the area with him that I was to learn the most interesting of news. We rode together east toward the Sanjon de Borregas, a ditch that marks the boundary between Aptos and Soquel. To our left was Loma Prieta and the vast forests of redwood, live oak, and madrona. A vast area to be owned by this soft-spoken man with still a lilt of the Dublin quays in his voice. His Martina was a woman to match most any man, and I envied him. The topic of Mesa was broached by Lodge who told me of the many duels and blood-letting he was responsible for. Only six months ago Mesa had been knifed in a public altercation with his mistress at a religious festival. Unfortunately the blubber had made it impossible for the puncture of any vital organ. Lodge noticed the glares we had exchanged and was warning me. I assured him that I would be vigilant and not ruin the *fandango* with his demise.*

Lodge mentioned that friends of his in Monterey and Los Angeles fear that war is near. They are leary of Pico and do not know what intrigues he may attempt with the British or the Russians. All in all this day has been the most rewarding since we sighted the valley of the Sacramento.

30TH JANUARY 1846

My life has become unsettled again. Fremont has returned to California. He has received permission from Sutter to winter in San Jose near the mission. I am anxious to see Alex, and all my friends, but their presence causes me a grave anxiety I can not fathom or put in words.

---

* Years later, long after California entered the Union, this same Mesa would come to a rather bizarre end on the streets of San Francisco. A diminutive French deaf-mute, armed only with a slingshot and mounted on a mule, would dispatch the corpulent officer in broad daylight. Fallon was to learn of the event and comment in a letter to his brother-in-law Henry Peck on May 14, 1860, that "someone ought to run that dwarf for Governor."

21st FEBRUARY 1846

Except for the normal reports and rumors all the news of Fremont had been put from my mind by this time. I was proceeding with the plans for the hotel and had had the honor of another visit to Rancho Soquel. On this evening I returned from a walk to the beach with Blackburn. The door to my house was slightly ajar. My only weapon was within. It was with a mixed feeling of surprise and relief that the figure stepped out of the doorway into the gathering dusk — Alex Godey.

22nd FEBRUARY 1846

By first dawn we had reached the camp near Gatos Ridge on the Santa Cruz range. The first man to greet me was Fremont, eyes deeper set than usual, and with that look the Delawares said was like a stone. Carson and Maxwell gave me great hugs, but it was Fremont who was most intense, questioning but friendly. He told me of his argument with Don Jose Dolores Pacheco, *alcalde* of San Jose, and about his rapid march out of the valley. Friends had told him of a ultimatum coming from General Castro. With an army of 200 at his back, Castro demands that this band of robbers and their captain leave California forthwith — it is plain that Fremont detests the thought of being forced to do anything. He wishes to communicate with Larkin* in Monterey.

I told him it could be done and that we had friends in Santa Cruz. The way I said <u>friends</u>, I believe, commited me to a course of action which until this moment I did not know I would take. Perhaps I always knew it, afterall.

6th MARCH 1846

Arrived at Sutter's fort with T. Shudden and continued on. Yesterday Fremont was officially ordered to leave the country. I will reach Bear Creek tomorrow and hopefully begin my work there.

---

* Thomas Larkin was American consul in Monterey, a prominent businessman, and almost certainly a spy and 'agent provacateur' for the Secretary of State of the United States, James Buchanan. Larkin would direct the famous messenger, Lieutenant Gillespie, to Fremont's camp in Northern California in a few months.

8TH MARCH 1846

Again at Sutter. The Captain is a bit nervous again. Word of the stalemate between Castro and Fremont's forty men at Gavilan Peak was made known to us. Beside the beautiful mission of San Juan I believe war will begin.*

15TH JUNE 1846

The Bear Flag has been raised in Sonoma. General Vallejo and the garrison are imprisoned. God knows what will be the result of this. Castro has several hundred men and is said to be arming the Indians. British and American ships are on the coast. Fremont is to the north. William Ide is in command and has written to me.

28TH JUNE 1846

Fremont is in Sonoma. It can only be a matter of time before they march south. I have consulted with Blackburn and we can count fifteen, including Daubenbiss, Weare, Sinclair, Peckham, Hecox and the Bennett brothers. Some express fear that the United States will stand clear and wish to wait for a sign from Fremont's men.

We intend to march on the Pueblo of San Jose as soon as possible. Word has reached here of the formation of a California Battalion to fight Castro. Its leader is John Fremont. Rifles are in short supply.

10TH JULY 1846

Encamped in the hills south of San Jose. Visited the ranch of Grove Cook. He was agog with the sound of the REPUBLIC OF CALIFORNIA.

---

* In this assessment Fallon was premature. The date is of interest. On the Texas frontier the U.S. Army under Zachary Taylor was preparing to march into Mexico. A real war was set to begin. In California however, the bombastic Castro allowed Fremont to exit into the San Joaquin Valley by the Pacheco Pass. The Americans set a leisurely gait north at 6 miles per day. They stopped at Bear Creek where Fallon would spend all of April. Whatever Fallon's mission was, apparently it terminated when Fremont struck out for Oregon and Fallon returned to Santa Cruz.

General Jose Castro

*General Mariano Vallejo shortly
after the Bear Flag Revolt.*

11TH JULY 1846

Entered the Pueblo early after dawn with nineteen men. No sign of General Castro. Drew my men up in front of the *juzgado* on Market Street. I am frankly amazed. Word has been sent to the naval commander at Yerba Buena that we are at his command.

My old friend Luis Peralta told me of the reason why the town was left undefended. Two days ago the word of the American occupation of Monterey reached here and Castro gathered his men on the plaza near the Church. He announced that he was going to Mexico! All who wished to follow him were welcome, the others could go home. With him he took the American Charles Weber who had written to me. Senor Peralta could scarcely hide a laugh in his voice. He remarked that Castro would surely return one day.* Still no flag. It is difficult to be a conqueror without one.

Following are the correspondence of mid-July, 1846.

FALLON TO MONTGOMERY, OFFERING TO RAISE U.S. FLAG
AT SAN JOSE
Pueblo St. Jose
July 12th, 1846

Capt. Mongomery. Sir,

I have arrived here with nineteen men, with the expectation of joining Capt. Fremont but he has not yet arrived here. I therefore send an express to you for orders what to do. We are at your command. If you wish we will hoist the American Flag and protect it here. I want an immediate answer if you can get horses to send the express back on & if you would send six guns and pistols, ammunition & c. I can get men to use them. Castro has gone down to the lower country last Wednesday and is traveling down as fast as he can. Governor Pico has been

---

* This remark was meant facetiously and led to a famous saying among the Californios of later years, *"cuando veulva Castro"* or "when Castro returns." This to signify an event of purely hypothetical and imaginary application or occurance.

trying to raise troops down at the lower Pueblo (Los Angeles) but can not get more than one hundred men. I have this news from an American direct from there. Mr. Charles Weber* has been taken prisoner by Castro and he is taking him down with him.

Capt. T. Fallon

P.S. I will remain here till I receive your answer. The Flag that was put up here was cut down before we came here, but I hope it never shall happen again.

T. F.

MONTGOMERY TO FALLON, ACCEPTING HIS OFFER

U.S. Ship Portsmouth
Yerba Buena   July 13th, 1846

Sir,

I have just received your letter of yesterday forwarded from the Pueblo St. Josephs, informing me that you had arrived there with nineteen men in the expectation of joining Capt. Fremont, but he having not yet arrived, you were induced to send an express to me for instructions what to do, as you were prepared to hoist the Flag of the United States, and to protect it if it should be my wish. In reply, Sir, permit me to say, that the United States & central Government of Mexico being at war that it is my wish, and that of the Commander in Chief at Monterey, to see the American Flag hoisted in every part of California where there shall be found sufficient force & patriotism honorably to sustain it, and if you think that your present force at the Pueblo with the accessions which I am told by the bearer of your letter, you are expecting, will be sufficient to that end, I would recommend to you by all means to do as you propose.

The six muskets & ammunition which you request me to furnish are at your disposal. The arms as a loan to be returned again when required or when you shall have been furnished with others, but as I have no means of sending them, I would advise you to send five of your men to Yerba Buena in order to receive them. The sixth being

---

* Charles Weber was a German immigrant who arrived in California a few years before Fallon. Although he held a commission in the Mexican militia, Weber actively conspired against the Government. His alleged capture, escape, and subsequent pecuniary motives while later procuring horses for Fremont's California Battalion are dealt with in detail in Dorothy Regnery's Battle of Santa Clara.

sent by your courier; I send you a receipt for the articles which you will please sign and return by the men whom you shall send for the arms.

I shall by the earliest opportunity notify the Commander in Chief, Commodore Sloat, now at Monterey, of your gratifying proposition, who will, I am persuaded, duly appreciate the spirit which dictated it.

The Flag of the United States is now flying at Sonoma, Bodega, & Sutters Fort, and will no doubt soon wave over the whole of California.

I shall be pleased to hear from you as opportunity's are afforded.

> I am Sir Respectfully
> Your Ob't Serv't.
> Signed. Jno. B. Montgomery
> Commanding U.S. Ship
> Portsmouth

To
  Capt. Thos. Fallon
  Pueblo of St. Josephs
  Upper California

P.S. I think it will be well, if it has not already been done, for you to call your company together and elect the necessary officers to command and direct them in order to have a more efficient organization, which has been done by a number of foreign residents at this place with excellent success.

> Respy. *J. B. M.*

MONTGOMERY TO SLOAT, REPORTING CONDITIONS AT YERBA BUENA

U.S. Ship Portsmouth
Yerba Buena
July 15th, 1846

Sir,

Your letter of the 12th inst. has just reached me forwarded by Mr. Stokes from the Pueblo, to whom I shall send this without any certainty of its being forwarded to you.

Having forwarded two communications by Mr. Die and Mr. Pitts your two first couriers, on Thursday and Sunday last, with information of a full compliance with your instructions of the 7th inst. which I feel confident, has duly reached you, I have now to report the safe return of my Launch on the 11th inst., after rather a severe passage of five days. In my first letter I informed you of the condition of the guns in the Fort at the entrance to the Bay, and that two brass eighteen pounders might be brought down from Sonoma, when they are of no manner of use, and be eligibly disposed of for the defence of this anchorage. I will now repeat that my Launch can transport said guns without difficulty, should you think proper to direct their removal. The two brass guns in the Fort (all that are worth anything) can I believe be recovered by boring new vents, and a long brass 12 has been already brought in from the Presidio, where it was buried. I am wholly at a loss, as to the whereabouts of Capt. Fremont — I wrote to him by an Officer (Purser Watmough) on the day of hoisting the Flag here, feeling certain that it would reach him almost immediately at the Pueblo San Joseph to which point I supposed him marching from the Sacramento, and since, hearing that he passed by another route on his way to Monterey, I concluded that he is now there without getting my letter. Everything is perfectly quiet here, and no apprehension whatever of disturbance from an enemy. Indeed, Sir, I am persuaded that no hostile opposition will be offered by the people of California to our occupation of the country. The American ship Vandalia arrived here yesterday, 18 days from Sn. Diego bringing news of a revolution in the south, by the American and Foreign residents, who have possessed themselves of the arms & munitions of that section, with a view to oppose Castro, whom it was reported was moving his forces against them, which must have been nearly simultaneous with the revolution at the north. I have the honor for your information to enclose copies of a letter received from Capt. Thos. Fallon and my answer. I perceive by your letter, that you were previously apprised of the state of affairs at Pueblo St. Joseph.

As Mr. Howard is expected here today or tomorrow from Monterey, I hope by him to receive later instructions from you. I am doing nothing to the old Fort except removing the brass guns, with a view to their recovery — as it is too far distant from my anchorage, & will require means not in my power to command at present to restore it to order. I will endeavour however to protect this anchorage and town — by such means as I have, against anything that shall oppose us.

We are all well — except myself having had a severe bilious attack of several days continuance, from which I am now recovering.

I have the honor to be
Sir, Your obt. Servt.
Jno. B. Montgomery
Commander

To

Commodore Jno. D. Sloat
Commanding the Naval Forces of the
U. States in the Pacific.

There are I am informed, a quantity of small arms of various discriptions at Sonoma which would probably be serviceable in arming the men now enrolling for the defense of our newly acquired teritory. Would it not be well to have an inventory taken of them. — I shall be happy to receive your instructions concerning them.

Resply

JBM

FALLON TO SLOAT, REPORTING ON SITUATION AT SAN JOSE

Pueblo St. Jose
July 16th 1846

Dear Sir,

Not having horses sufficiently fresh to carry us to Capt. Fremont's camp and the Justice having need of a small force at this place to enable him to enforce the laws, we will with your permission, stop at this place until such time as we are ordered on active service. There is a number of lawless characters in the vicinity of this place (principally foreigners) who have taken an active part with Gen. Castro in all underhand measures to annoy the Americans here before we had any protection from our government. Two of them we were in search of today. The man who had our fellow citizen Mr. Weber taken. We have not succeeded in capturing them as yet, but we will I have no doubt. Should it meet your views we would wish you to arm the six men of our company who accompanied Lieutenant Galespie* to Monterey and have them placed under the one you think most competent and sent back. I am happy to inform you we have (according to your wishes) hoisted the star spangled banner on the 14th Inst., and we hope it may wave & dispense its blessings throughout this country. We will have our company full in a few days when we will report to you.

We have the honor to
to remain &c
Thos. Fallon, Capt.
W. Blackburn, Liet.

* Archibald Gillespie, was a pivotal figure in this era. An officer in the U.S. Marine Corps, he made the long journey from Washington, D.C. across northern Mexico to California in this year with dispatches. Some went to Larkin in Monterey, another caused Fremont to return south from Oregon and join the Bear Flag affair. Gillespie served as adjutant and second in command of the California Battalion.

14TH JULY 1846

For form sake I have arrested the *alcalde*, Dolores Pacheco, and obtained the keys to the archives. Having received a flag from Commodore Sloat, we proceeded to raise it over the Pueblo at the *juzgado* near El Dorado Street. A small crowd attended the ceremony. Surrendered the keys to archives to James Stokes. Intend to proceed to Mission San Juan Bautista.

17TH JULY 1846   PASS OF SAN JUAN

Arrived and joined with Fremont's California Battalion. Some urge us to take a name such as Fauntleroy's Leather A Dragoons, so called for the leather on the seats and knees of their pants. I tell them what we wear on our pants would scarce make a fiercesome name.

Learned for the first time of the death of Basil Lajeunesse, the old *voyageur*. He was killed by Klamath Indians one dawn, his skull split with a tomahawk. Fremont had posted no guard on the mentioned night. Carson and Godey enacted a grim vengence on the miscreants.

Castro has buried cannons and again fled south.

19TH JULY 1846   MONTEREY

Entered the old capital at the head of the legion of California. We must make a sight. 250 of us with broad-brimmed hats, buckskin shirts, moccasins and long beards and hair.

Even Fremont is more sunburnt than usual, and always surrounded by his five Delaware bodyguards. Most of us carry Hall or Hawkens across our pommell and Bowie knives and pistols adorn every belt.

23RD JULY 1846

Fremont is made a major by Admiral Stockton. Stockton had replaced the overly cautious Sloat and incorporated the California Battalion under his command. Embark on the sloop, Cyane, Monday, to cut off Castro's retreat. At last we may come to grips with the rogue.

The California Battalion moving south from Monterey in 1846

One of the loyal Delaware bodyguards.

13TH AUGUST 1846

There has been little time for writing. Everyone, notably Carson, was sick with the heavy swells and high winds before we reached San Diego. Five days ago we proceeded to the lower pueblo of Los Angeles with 120 men. Captain Gillespie with Godey are left to garrison San Diego. Both Pio and Andres Pico are in hiding. Castro is nowhere.

Stockton rendezvous with us outside pueblo. The day is terrible warm. A band played Hail Columbia as we entered unopposed. Here is another place for General Castro to return to . . .

18TH AUGUST 1846   SANTA BARBARA

We go north. Talbot and ten men are to be left here as garrison. News reaches us here of 1000 Walla Walla Indians under their chief Yellow Serpent raiding the Sacramento. Ned Kern is there alone.

25TH SEPTEMBER 1846   NEW HELVITIA

There is no war in this land. Kern feels a fool. We support the feeling.

28TH SEPTEMBER 1846

Gillespie has been attacked in the lower pueblo. I worry about Godey. Talbot has fled Santa Barbara. The whole province is alive. Fremont has sent word to meet him at Sonoma or San Juan. How have these disasters transpired?

14TH OCTOBER 1846

Many joined at Sutter's Fort. Even the ghost Indians, Chief Trukee and his brother Pancho of the Pyramid Lake Paiutes. We are over 400 strong, one bugle, two cannons, an ammunition wagon and 1900 head of horses and mules. Horses everywhere. Weber gave vouchers to friends and took without compensation from enemies. I hope he can tell the difference.

15TH NOVEMBER 1846

A week of drills has left us more confused than before. Fremont announced that the trek south is to begin. The season is very rainy. Wet. Cold. I am anxious to go south but we can only cover six or eight miles a day in this condition. The men grumble.

14TH DECEMBER 1846

We have been traveling very near to the coast. The weather is still chilly and the drizzle constant. There are war ships to our right and for once I wish I was on one.

For the second day in a row we see whale spouts to the sea side. Only beef to eat. We approach San Luis Obispo. From the height above the mission we can see the tiled roofs. We wonder if the enemy is near. Raining still.

15TH DECEMBER 1846

There is no enemy near the mission. Save one perhaps. Totoi Pico, a Californio who fought at the Battle of Natividad and was parolled, has been taken. He carries dispatches. Dreadful news. At San Pascual the Army of the West under General Kearny has been defeated by Andres Pico's lancers. Lieutenant Gillespie is reported killed. Fremont ordered the prisoner executed.

17TH DECEMBER 1846

Execution day. Captain Owen brings Senora Pico to the Major's tent. The sentence is to be commuted. Fremont is beginning to think more and more clearly.

27TH DECEMBER 1846

We crossed the San Marcus Pass in a river of mud and water. Are nearing Santa Barbara thru the San Ynez mountains. Over 100 horses have died since we began. At 2:00 in the afternoon we ride thru the town. I do not feel we look the part of conquerors. Orders have been issued to respect all private property. Four paroles are issued.

1ST JANUARY 1847

Another new year. Los Angeles has fallen. The only question is which way will Pico flee.

By the end of this month the southern war will be ended. Learn that Gillespie is only wounded. A lance pierced his lung but Carson brought him to succor. Godey is not hurt.

General Stephen Watts Kearny, Commander of the Army of the West.

10TH JANUARY 1847   MISSION SAN FERNANDO

At a small ranch house north of the Cahuenga Pass, Andres Pico has surrendered and accepted terms. His parole is made. I talk briefly to him of friends in San Jose. He smiles on one side of his mouth as is his habit. Fremont's Proclamation is read to the assembled men.

"Put an end to war and to the feeling of war". With plumes and feathers we enter Los Angeles. Raining still. My old comrades seem never to change. Alex and Maxwell. How many days we spent together. For me it is time to return home.

Ed.: *Although there were plans for a Pacific invasion of Mexico, events were moving to a speedy conclusion there also. Mexico City was soon taken and the war ended. In northern California, a battle was fought in this same month of January 1847, in the mustard field west of the Santa Clara mission. With only a few injuries, the Californios were driven from the field. So ended a war which the* Encyclopedia Americana *dismisses as one in which "Everywhere success attended the arms of the United States. Perhaps it was the first war in history lasting two years, in which no defeat was sustained by one party, and no victory by the other." A clever phrase. If only the participants of San Pascual could have seen it with such prescience.*

III

The City

5TH APRIL 1847

AFFAIRS IN SANTA Cruz are well. My absence has seen the success of many of my ventures. Perhaps I should leave more frequently. The California Battalion was formally disbanded this month. Many of the men are very bitter. I have entered a claim for $283.00 but hold little hope for its settlement.

Mr. Lodge questioned me about the sincerity of the guarantees of religious freedom and rights of property. I have informed him that all to my knowledge will be provided and compensation for any goods confiscated. I hope that this is so. The decision to protect them in their property is a wise one. They have suffered through many changes of authority. We must convince them this is just another. There is said to be much confusion beween Fremont and General Kearny in the south. Stockton is gone.

12TH APRIL 1847   NEW HELVITIA

The fort is a scene of constant riot. More ragged survivors of the emigrant train have come in. They tell the most bloody tales. Captain Kern is determined to have another try at a rescue. He has asked me to lead a party to their aid. Much was related to me by James Reed of this Donner Expedition. He commanded the second relief into the mountains. There were many young children. Dozens have died. When Sutter sent mules loaded with beef and two Indians, they ate both the beef and the Indians. This is hard to believe. Foster and Rhodes have volunteered to accompany me.

15TH APRIL 1847

Left Johnson's ranch and arrived at the lower end of Bear Valley. Hung up our saddles and sent the horses back to be returned in ten days time. The snow is 2-3 feet as our journey began. Our provisions are for ten days. We have made 23 miles. The snow is ten feet deep.

17TH APRIL 1847

Reached the cabins near noon. Inside the cabin we were presented a horrible scene. Human bodies were scattered everywhere — legs, arms, skulls in mutilated states. One body supposed to be that of Mrs. Eddy lay near the entrance, the limbs severed off, and a frightful gash in the skull.

All seemed dead. A painful stillness was on the land. A sudden shout broke out and we raced to see three Indians fleeing, leaving behind a bow and arrow. We searched the cabins for two hours. Still no sign of Mrs. Donner or Keseberg who have been reported alive.

Eight miles over the mountains we approached the camp of Jacob Donner. Property of every description—books, calicoes, tea, coffee, shoes, percussion caps, furniture is scattered everywhere in the water. At the mouth of the tent stood a large iron kettle — full of human flesh. Nearby we found what we believe is the body of George Donner—the skull is split and the brain has been extracted.

There are tracks in the snow close at hand. Made with boots. A leg of a bullock is found that had been shot in the winter and snowed upon before it could be dressed. The meat is sound and good, but I must admit my appetite is not. We camped for the night.

19TH APRIL 1847

This morning Foster and Rhodes and myself started for the higher cabins. We have lost the trail of the boots. Knowing that the Donners had a considerable sum of money, we left behind three men to search thoroughly. Snow is melting rapidly. The first cabin we entered presents another bizarre sight—Keseberg was lying down amid bones and beside him a large pan full of fresh liver. Mrs. Donner and the others were all dead he informed us. She had been forced to sleep out and had froze. He said he ate her body and found her flesh the best he had ever tasted. Her body provided him with four pounds of fat. There is no trace of Mrs. Murphy, Foster's mother-in-law. After a search gold was found concealed in Keseberg's waistcoat. Further exploration revealed a brace of pistols and more gold totaling near $400.

Rhodes wishes to kill him on the spot. I have heard of cannibals before, but it never hit home to me. Carson used to say in earnest that in starving times, don't walk in front of old Bill Williams.*

20TH APRIL 1847

We all started for Bear Valley with packs of 100 pounds each. Provisions are low. I confronted Keseberg and he again protested that he had no further money. I choose words designed to shock this hideous creature. "Keseberg, you know well where Donner's money is, and damm you, you shall tell me! I am not going to multiply word with you or say but little about it. Bring me that rope!"

I bent the rope around his neck and tightened the cord. He cried out that he would tell me if I would only release him. I then permitted him to arise. Rhodes and Tucker accompanied him back the ten miles to camp to find the hidden treasure.

In their absence we moved all our packs on the lower end of the lake, and made all ready for a start when they should return. Found the body of young Murphy. Dead about three months.

The cache of Keseberg resulted in a find of only $273.00. Rhodes says with great anger that he had to listen to the babbling of the cannibal over the merits of liver—too dry—brains and lights. He alternated this with appeals to God to forgive him and hopes that he may reach heaven. It is hard to not hate this beast. I wish that Hastings** could have provided him with one of those meals.

21ST APRIL 1847

Started for Bear Valley this morning. Found the snow from six to eight feet deep. Camped at Yuma River*** for the night. On the next day we will cover the eighteen miles to the Bear.

---

* A contemporary mountain man. He was credited years after this entry with guiding the disastrous Fourth Fremont expedition into the San Juan Mountains, and has been violently berated by many annalists.

**This refers to Landsford Hastings, early pioneer and author who helped to popularize California with his writings. He envisioned himself a Sam Houston-type who would help win a new land. With the publication of an Emigrants Guide to Oregon and California . . . all the information necessary to the equipment, supplies, and method of travel to those countries, (Cincinatti, 1845), he unwittingly set the stage for the Donner disaster. It was a basic premise of this book to strike out south of Salt Lake, a shortcut, across the Humboldt Sink and save time.This book had a wide readership and was as influential as Fremont's Report of the 1842 Expedition. Fremont had refused to endorse the Humboldt route; Fallon thought it to be little short of murder.

*** Probably Yuba River.

25TH APRIL 1847

Moved to the lower end of the valley and met our horses. Came in.

Ed.: The controversy surrounding the various relief expeditions to the Donner Party continue unabated to this day. Motivations are difficult to determine but it was well known that Mrs. Murphy reputedly told the second relief party she would pay $500 for help. Rumors of great wealth on the train abounded and the search for money was certainly, as his Journal indicated, in the heads of Fallon's men. Captain Kern hired men for this party at $1½ per diem and other rescuers had received a bounty for "saved pilgrims." Fallon and Foster reportedly served without compensation.

In June of 1847 the company of General Kearny traveling east with John Fremont under arrest for insubordination, stopped at this spot of tragedy. According to Edwin Bryant, Captain George Donner's body was found neatly laid out. The California Star later carried both Fallon's and Bryant's versions and the results were predictably inconclusive. According to oral history, a trial was held before Alcalde Sinclair and resulted in a courtesy judgement of $1.00 against Captain Fallon in Keseberg's favor. All records have long since been destroyed. The mists and snows descend on this last chapter of the ill-fated venture. Of the 87 members of the original Donner Party, forty were to die. The entire family of James Frazier Reed, a contemporary of Captain Fallon, was saved and settled in San Jose where their names commemorate numerous streets, i.e., Reed, Margaret, Virginia, Keyes.

23RD SEPTEMBER 1847   NEW HELVITIA

The summer and spring of this year have come and gone swiftly. Most of my time has been divided between Santa Cruz and San Jose. Adna Hecox and I have been successful in many enterprises. Elihu Anthony's new blacksmith shop will be completed by the first of the year. We have wonderful plans for the future. Savage is with me now. We are going to join Marshall* at the sawmill on the American.

30TH SEPTEMBER 1847

Murphy and I are to return to the coast at first light. The trip was productive.

---

* James Marshall was a long-time employee of Sutter and a man with whom Fallon dealt numerous times. In a few months his discovery of gold in January of 1848 would rock the nation and alter forever the fortunes of Captain Sutter and indeed the whole world.

27TH NOVEMBER 1847   SANTA CRUZ

The village is very much awake today. The *alcalde*, my former lieutenant, Blackburn, has made a Solomon-like judgement. A young boy has been apprehended while cutting off the tail of a horse. Good William has ordered the boy's head shaved. I find this type of judgement more to my liking than the twelve lashes he laid on the Mexican last week for fighting. Few friends are made with a whip.

12TH FEBRUARY 1848

It has been a new year crammed with event. In Washington, John Fremont was adjudged guilty by the Army bootlickers. Even old Senator Benton could not fight off the bastards once they sensed his blood. Any man with as great a destiny to fulfill as Fremont can expect to attract many enemies. For now they have the poor man in an awkward spot. One would think that the conclusion of the Treaty of Guadalupe Hidalgo confirming all these rich new lands to the United States would have caused them to give due to a man who was so responsible for these great gains. Such was not to be.

20TH FEBRUARY 1848

After long persuasions Blackburn has agreed to sell me the quarter league of land on the eastern chalk bluff overlooking the San Lorenzo River. It is a piece of ground where I would like to build a house sometime. A married man with property should have a fine house for his family.

22ND FEBRUARY 1848

Called to the home of Michael and Martina Lodge at the Rancho Soquel. Had the honor to walk a short way to the river with the Dona and Maria del Carmen or Carmel as they call her. She has the beautiful full face of an Irish lady and the dark shades of her mother. The old sand road back home to the Mission plaza was very short this evening. My thoughts are far away.

28TH FEBRUARY 1848

Inspected the mill on the Soquel River with Hecox and Michael Lodge. Hecox is soon to construct a similar building on Rancho Zayante for Isaac Graham. Lodge is quite specific to warn against this *cholo,* who only made money on another's sorrow, and hired his rifle to anyone with the right amount of gold. Adna will take this advice. I have asked him to send it no further for Graham is indeed a strange and violent fellow.

30TH MAY 1848

It is very hard to reconcile. Gold is said to have been found in great quantities on the American Fork near Sutter's sawmill. All the days I have spent in those digs and I am now so far away — in the wrong place.

2ND JUNE 1848

This is to be a summer of decision for me. I have discussed the matter with Lodge and Blackburn, Anthony and Hecox. There is a great rush of humanity to go to the hills. It is said that Yerba Buena has only twenty souls in residence. San Jose and Monterey are also near deserted. The one sure way to reap a fortune from this affair is to provide for the insensibility of all the others. We will form a junta to sell goods — sundries, mules, horses, picks. In this way we shall profit whether there is a fortune in the ground or not. I surely think the second condition will prevail.

1ST SEPTEMBER, 1848

The summer has passed with the speed of a rushing fire. Our venture in the gold fields are very happy. Hecox has returned with over $2200 on an investment of only $800. My trip in July with the picks made from ships bolts was especially fruitful. For each pick I have asked and received three ounces of gold. Some fool had bought a goldometer even. All the saddles were sold, too. The three mules fetched a very high price from two Englishmen. Encountered Blackburn near the outer fork. There was no luck in his digging. I believe he is very sorry to have resigned as *alcalde* for this adventure.

28TH DECEMBER 1848

Today camped near the Mission of San Jose. My long journey was nearly cut short. I carried with me $2500.00 for the purchase of cattle for my friend Michael Lodge. At dusk three men rode into our camp and took supper with us. The conversation proceeded in such a manner that my guard was raised. I felt sure that they would attempt harm to the servant and me. With a curious lack of luck my pistol was not working and I began to tell of my dry digging and the desire to swap my horse for a *carreta* in the pueblo. I have, it seems, a talent for lying. The men rode off after a smoke. My judgement is correct.

3RD JANUARY 1849

Three men were hung today west of the pueblo of San Jose for the murder of two Germans. It is the same three.

20TH JANUARY 1849   SANTA CRUZ

The mission padre, Real, is being moved to the Santa Clara de Asis Mission. Lodge has helped me to procure the lease of the Mission orchard. We walked down Willow Street to the swamps and on to the beach. Talk ranged from Ireland to Mexico. Hecox met us near the western cliffs where I often go. The new *alcalde* wears his office a bit heavily. When Blackburn returns he may wear it no longer.

20TH FEBRUARY 1849

Since I left St. Vrain's the need to find something has been foremost in my mind. Today it has been agreed that Carmel Lodge will become my wife in the late spring. I am sure that now this is my home. My fortune is nearing two score thousand dollars, and we have plans for two new buildings, one on the plaza, the other near Anthony's foundry fronting the *potrero* on the flat.

17TH MAY 1849

The ceremony was of great beauty. All of the old Spanish families were present. It was a wonderful amalgam of the new order with the past. Fremont, Godey and Maxwell were to come, but have heard nothing. Blackburn stood for me while three of the Lodge sisters preceded the bride. I had caught sight of her the day before with Martina, both dressed in black, headed toward the Mission. What this girl of 18 could confess to the old padre I could hardly guess. At the church altar my next vision was of an angel in white, spotless and a

45

Carmel Lodge Fallon

gold chain around her neck — how fortunate I am in this beautiful girl.

The dancing lasted well into the morning and old Ricardo said that no wedding in recent memory could exceed its splendor. While my mind was clear it seemed a special *fandango*.

❈   ❈   ❈

31st DECEMBER 1849

It was a summer and fall to remember this year. Much time was spent on the Rancho, and Carmel and I would often take long walks on our own land beside the San Lorenzo and speak of the years ahead. Our family and the house we would build facing the long strand rolling beyond the river estuary.

Only once did the happiness pale. Lodge, Blackburn and I journeyed to San Jose for the first session of the Legislature. The trip should have been saved. The Californios call these *Extrangeros commisionados, the Ayuntamiento de mil bebidas.** They seem more interested in drink and song than in the job of governing this land. Someone must see that schools are provided, a local militia established, the boundaries set, and provisions for public buildings made. Burnett is here and may be against those who wish to outlaw slavery in the Territory. The winter was very wet but this bug should not have come from under the rock where he was.

Had a long visit with Don Luis Peralta, my friend. He asked that we give his respects to Martina, and told the story of how he and Joaquin Castro, her father, had made the overland trek from Tubac as young boys. Captain De Anza was spoken of gloriously. I had heard it before but Don Luis added a nice touch, and extra flair here and there. While there, General Vallejo, the present Senator, paid a visit. I heard much of this man but never had seen him. For such a scholar he carried not a book or even a scrap of paper.**

---

* Legislature of the Thousand Drinks, a well-known derisive term.

**The reference is to the large library which Mariano Vallejo owned. His pride in it was legend and he had even duelled the far reaching minions of the Inquisition to maintain it unabridged and uncensored. For a generation the General had been a power in California, aligned now with Castro, then with Alvarado, always being the balance of power. In June of 1846 he was a prisoner of the Bear Flaggers, and in chains at Sutter's Fort. In 1849 he was a State Senator. He had the uncanny ability to land on his feet. Along with his reputation as an omniverous reader was his fecundity. A large family of sixteen with such classical names as Napoleon, Plutarco, Andronico and Platon, helped control his vast interests. Later, in the fight to return the State capital to San Jose, Fallon would joust briefly with Vallejo and utter a much quoted insult: "With the General's habits for windy speeches and nocturnal reading, it is a wonder that the size of his family is so great."

47

Antonio Pico and Pacheco were by after supper. The adobe of Peralta is slightly north of the Alameda, fast to the *acequia* that flows to the Guadalupe Creek. There is no disagreeable fog here as in Santa Cruz. Wild mustard grows in profusion on the plain to the creek and the orchard is as beautiful and productive as any in the land. I will come again to this spot. Before I left, Don Luis took me aside and in a moment of confidence told me not to put my faith in gold but in the land. Of his sons and his Rancho San Antonio he expresses great fears.* "Keep the land, Don Tomas, he said firmly, keep it always." This was a rare honor. I will be happy to see mission hill in Santa Cruz tomorrow.

10TH JANUARY 1850

The new year will come with tears this time. Michael Lodge left for Sutter's Fort three weeks ago. Nothing has been seen there of him. I fear him gone.

16TH JANUARY 1850

The world moves ahead. A hardy city is blooming on the mission plaza and below on the flats. Blackburn has the Eagle Hotel newly painted and across the Adobe Street toward the mission wall I have added rooms to my shop and residence. It is now a magnificent story and a half of good wood with an outside stairway to boot. Together we will have the two finest hotels in the county. We will name the street in front of us Emmett after Bold Robert Emmett, the Irish patriot. I know John Jennings would like that honor. It is a strange way to commemorate a poor fool who led twelve men up a Dublin street and then was hung, drawn and quartered into legend. "Bold Robert," indeed. Anthony had laid out three other buildings on the flat, on Main Street and Willow beneath mission hill and beyond his foundry. One day buildings will reach from Emmett through the willow path to the strand — one day soon.

16TH MARCH 1850

A single entry here. Maria de los Angeles Fallon was born today. My little Mary.

---

* Rancho San Antonio was the large holding of Don Luis, administered by his four sons. It comprised over 44,000 acres and the present East Bay cities of Berkeley, Oakland, Emoryville, San Leandro, et. al. The former *commissionado* died in 1851 in the small two room adobe where he had always lived. The home is still standing on St. John Street, San Jose.

SANTA CRUZ
The site of the first pier. The Mission is seen in the distance.

Santa Cruz of the 1870's The Mission Plaza is on the left center and the bluffs at the mouth of the San Lorenzo River are in the center foreground.

Santa Cruz. At the base of the Mission Plaza, the intersection of the present-day Front and Pacific Garden Mall, the willow-lined avenue of the padres.

28TH APRIL 1850

The great election is over. The State Constitution is working. We will be in the Union soon. John Fremont is to take up his role in Washington as Senator. It is said that if anyone can uncompromise that city, it is John C.* Over 213 votes were cast in our little hamlet. A letter from San Jose informs me that the vote for annexation was 567-0. John Burnett was elected Governor last November with only 516 votes. He is likely searching the pueblo for 51 men to wreak his vengeance. One term as Governor should do that deed well enough.

4TH JUNE 1850

A large gathering was held at Rancho Soquel this day. Something was to be expected by the tenor of the Dona for some months past. The priest was by her side through the whole day. At mid-noon we were called together. Martina Castro spoke in a low voice with her eyes closed, of that day when she had claimed all this land from bluff to bluff, and from the foothills to the sea. Then she spoke the sentence I was to hear so many times after, even unto my dreams — "I walked on the land, pulled up grass, threw handfulls of earth, broke off branches, and cast stones to the four winds."** This last was chanted in a rhythmic fashion. All this land was for the glory of God and for her family, she said.

A large, hand-etched document was then produced by the priest which divided Rancho Soquel and the Soquel Augmenta into ninths. One for each of the children and one reserved to her. It was an epic thing. In one stroke Carmel and I had become one of the largest land owners in all of California. Our share lay west of the creek and north of the road to Monterey. Thomas Fallon of County Cork had become one of the landed aristocracy of old California.

Ed.: *The Soquel Rancho was formally subdivided and the one-ninths distributed on 29 August 1850.*

---

* The Great Compromise of 1850 was enacted that year. The tenuous balance of slave and free was maintained. On February 5, 1850, the old masters Henry Clay, Daniel Webster, John Calhoun, and Thomas Hart Benton balanced the scales and bought a little time for the Union. It would not last. Fremont was a well-known abolitionist who had been elected at the First Legislature months previously.

** This corresponds very closely to the acts of possession described by the noted historian, Hubert Howe Bancroft in his epic works. A word is changed here and there but the meaning and tradition are identical.

Martina Castro Lodge

2ND MARCH 1851

Today the baptism of my first son — Jose Carlos Fallon. The name of my father and of the man who guided me to this California land, John Charles Fremont. Dona Martina did not attend the christening. Carmel is very excited and upset. She speaks so rapidly at times like this that her Spanish is hard for me to follow. It makes the child cry also.

10TH MARCH 1851

I begin to dispise the name Soquel. There is one argument after another about which land is which — trees, water, sand — soon even the air and the birds that fly in it will be an object of contention. I wish to God we had never received our part of the Rancho. The legislature is a vicious farce. One newspaper I have read called them a perfect turn. I have saved this article: "They are an infamous, ignorant, drunken, rowdy, perjured and traitorous body of men." It is a random sampling and none too far-fetched.

9TH APRIL 1851

Bought a fine parcel of land north of the mission near the river. It is the old *potrero*. Paid $800.00 and feel quite confident in my prospects there.

10TH NOVEMBER 1851

Purchased half interest in the Arroyo de Ballena for $1370.00. Over 480 acres are there.

12TH FEBRUARY 1852

No word has been received of my desire to divide my holdings for the children. If only U.S. law allowed a simple *sobrante* grant my task would be simple. The litigation and courts are constant in the Soquel matter. It was always tradition to grant to a spot on the hill where Don Joaquin or Don Raphael sat on his horse. In their blessed simplicity they forgot that horses move, at least ones that I do not bet on. The priest plays a foul part in the dispute, I fear. All is entered and sent to the Land Court. Lawyers and priests are a bad combination. Even my old orchard lease is being brought to question. Martina treats Carmel and I with some dispatch. The children are likewise corrected many, many times.

Ed.: To settle the frightful confusion in land tenure following the American occupation, a Land Commission was authorized by the U.S. Congress in 1851. Great fortunes were made and lost by its decisions, many of which were appealed and counter-appealed for well over a decade. The inability to transfer sound title was an additional concomitant of instability in a land with an ever-growing population, all hungry for places of their own.

21st MARCH 1852

Lawyer Peckham is trying to work out some accomodation on the orchard. In the rancho matter we are also at a great loss. Dona Martina is suing several of us — Carmel, Antonio and her husband, Henry Peck — God only knows where it will end. That priest I feel is poisoning her against each of the children in turn.

3rd APRIL 1852

Long conferences have done little help. The matter is sure to end in a disasterous action in court. Carmel is upset and ready to do a drastic turn.

9th JUNE 1852

It is getting so the people in California will soon outnumber the cattle. Papers report each day of wagons leaving Council Bluffs or Westport. Thirty thousand are said to have made the journey in the last year from these two alone. Fort Kearny is full of activity. Godey writes from Los Angeles that he sees no end to the hordes of people coming across the land. The blasted gold I fear was only the start of a wave that will sweep many of us to more peaceful climes.

A man spoke to me today of the fields of waist high sedge grass in Texas, and of the deep black soil. A land where the cedar brakes are as perfect as anywhere. It is said to be a very settled state of affairs since after the war.

10th JUNE 1852

We have set matters in motion today from which we can not retreat. We would scarce want such a decision. No more is possible with the old woman and the priest. I have conferred at great length with Carmel. The decision is made to dispose of all holdings and depart for Texas in as quick a manner as prudence allows. A year or two may pass but I will not continue here in this climate of hate and fear. I must do the best for Carmel and the little ones. They hung the Scotsman today at the beach for the shooting at the Santa Cruz House.

54

18TH OCTOBER 1852

The negotiations with the county of Santa Cruz have come to a good resolve. The price of $3500.00 has been agreed to for the purchase of my hotel fronting the mission plaza — it is to be the new Court house of the county. Quite a fine deal. Anthony has concluded the note with Majors also this month. Blackburn wishes that I join him in potato fields in the Neary Lagoon bottomland where his home is. From there it is only a short distance to the Anthony's pier constructed on Rocky beach and the connection with the schooners north.* I think that this Irishman has seen far too many potatoes and far too much strife in this land. Texas is beckoning.

12TH APRIL 1853

The steamer Jenny Lind exploded outside of Alviso with 150 souls aboard. Charles White and Hoppe are killed. Many are horribly burned and mutilated.

1ST AUGUST 1853

Our portion of the Rancho today was disposed to Joseph Parrish. So ends a condition that should never have begun. The Land Judges can now do their worst!

5TH OCTOBER 1853

Made inquiries of passage to New Orleans and then on to Texas. Many have used the bark Canton to Panama, steerage at $50 and across the isthmus on foot or mule. The danger of disease is too great and with a wife and three children** I must be prudent. I have booked passage on a steamer for all of us. We leave the 16th of October and the journey should take 50 or 60 days. I am so glad to be leaving my problems behind — the law suits, courts, and the terrible crime — it is a land where murder and robbery have become the rule, not an exception. It is all one can do to avoid the brigands on the local roads and near the gold fields where poor Michael Lodge was assaulted, it is nearly impossible to avoid death and disaster. The Government is powerless. Conditions can only lead to a total breakdown of all civilization. Times are rough indeed and I fear that my exit is none too soon.

* The first pier in Santa Cruz was on the site of today's Dream Inn, and consisted of a long chute down from the cliffs to the waiting schooners at sea. William Blackburn's home still stands at 101 Cedar Street, near the lagoon that was so good to him.

** Although the Pastoral Records of the Diocese of Monterey show no record of it, Fallon and his wife, Carmel, likely became the parents of another child before the journey to Texas. The total of children was three in October, of 1853.

Ed.: Fallon could have been speaking in the late Twentieth Century instead of 1853, but the topic of lawlessness was the major topic of the day. The noted California historian, Julian Dana, in his book <u>Sutter</u> gave the grim statistics of 4200 murders, 1200 in San Francisco alone, in the years 1849-1859. These are figures with which even New York City or Detroit of today would be horrified. The population was unstable, transient, male, and lusting for gold: fatal ingredients, as any sociologist would note.

6TH OCTOBER 1853

Received a letter from my brother-in-law, Henry Peck. The old woman* has stopped the suit against her children. I have advised him to act as my agent in Santa Cruz during my absence. He is to tell Mr. Peckham to stop all proceedings against her in my case. The costs are to be settled by the money collected from Byrd and Majors. Tracy, Wright and Ricardo's note is to be paid by the first of December.

Had to assure Peck that his fear that my agent might sue on the notes I have of his are foolishness. They are in a safe with orders to do nothing. I told him that I was rather surprised that he should think I would do otherwise.

7TH OCTOBER 1853

The pot-gutted Jesuit priest has entered suit against me here for $2500 dollars. He has done it to annoy me as I am at the point of leaving, but he might just as well amuse himself in some other way — he can do nothing — we have got him by the nuts. Advised Peck to contact my lawyers, Mr. Peachy of the firm of Halleck, Peachy and Billings, the best lawyers in the City.

8TH OCTOBER 1853

In an attempt to extort some money out of me, the priest has garnished some money of mine in the bank. Poor fool. He is most damnably mistaken. This suit is the testing suit and after it's decided I will not have any more trouble.

9TH OCTOBER 1853

Have succeeded in getting the garnishment released by giving security. I am rather pleased that the suit has been brought against me before I left. This case won't interfere a particle in my arrangements. I will be off on the steamer at 9 o'clock Sunday morning. Of this there is no doubt.

* Dona Martina Castro, sobriquet from Fallon.

The Explosion of the Steamboat Jenny Lind, 1853

Alex Godey in his "civilized" years

10TH OCTOBER 1853

This is a week of many entries. The business of settling my affairs is irksome, but I feel quite good. I will have a chance of getting costs and damages. I can come down on the priest's board men. I am not the least uneasy as to the result of this suit. Everythting, all my affairs are in order.

12TH OCTOBER 1853   SAN FRANCISCO

This is a City where all of mankind will pass by if you wait for them. I have seen Kit Carson and Hatchey and Tim Goode and Maxwell and Alex Godey. All here but they are now gone to New Mexico and Texas after more cattle and sheep. Except Godey who has gone to his farm near St. Barbara. With that group I finally feel safe and comfortable on a simple walk. Even the "Hounds of Sydney"* would avoid that party. In Texas we may join again.

15TH OCTOBER 1853

I have my business here safe and snug but I have to pay such a percentage for everything done here that it may be to my advantage to come here next Spring and wind up my affairs myself. I will come back next springtime.

16TH OCTOBER 1853

Evening on the Steamer. Sailing from the harbor I felt a very great loss. The California that I love has changed. Emigrating again is not what I ever wanted. Once in a lifetime is enough. I cannot help but think of the harbor in Cork City so many years ago. This time it is I who bring the family as my mother and father brought me to a new life. For them I will make a fresh new start in Texas. It will be a good home for Carmel and my three angels. Move swiftly.

---

* A local gang of cutthroats and robbers.

I V

The Mind

2ND APRIL 1854   SAN FRANCISCO

IT IS WITH a great bewilderment that I once more begin an entry in my Journal. For half a year I have not felt a need to record anything of the happenings of my life. Terrible things have transpired.* My heart is sick. At times it is impossible to convey an idea by words of what I suffer. All my bright hopes are gone. Yet I suppose time will bring brighter days. The only consolation I now have is the affection of my wife and the sympathies of a few true friends. At times my heart almost fails me but I try and rally for I know it won't do to give up. I must go ahead. I must go ahead.

11TH APRIL 1854

I am to let Mr. Majors have some money on bond and mortgage of one ninth of the Soquel ranch. The part that said Majors and Sinclair owns. Peckham is to attend to it. The mortgage is to be for six months for two thousand dollars bearing a monthly interest of 3½% until paid. Have instructed Peck in Santa Cruz to get the recorder's certificate that the premises is unencumbered and that there are no judgements recorded against either of them. Majors is to pay all expenses for the making out papers as is the custom. I hope they remember to put the words "until paid" in the mortgage.

---

* In New Orleans the three young children of Thomas and Carmel unexplainably died. The oldest would have been about 3½ years; the boy, Joseph Charles, 2½ years. The dread killer cholera was prevalent in the port cities and typhoid is also a likely candidate for the cause of death.

1st MAY 1854

Peck is still concerned about the money he owes me. Poor Antonia. With such a worrying husband she will surely be a young widow. Again I have advised him not to concern himself about these personal notes.

Often the thought of purchasing our own share of the Rancho crosses my mind. I may search for a place to suit me between here and San Jose or near San Jose Mission. My wife, Carmel, is in fine health at present and I think the trip to San Jose will help both her and myself. On her account I wish a place in Santa Cruz but I don't like to bring her in contact with the old woman. If it was not for that infernal priest and the old woman I would not have taken my family with me to the States. I was afraid to leave them.

31st MAY 1854

I have purchased a fine piece of property in San Jose from Mr. Yates. It is on the street connecting San Pedro and Market, formerly owned by Davidson. Pacheco is the name and I may find new fortunes in a shop there. It is only a few steps from the *juzgado* where the flag was raised by us in 1846.

21st JUNE 1854   SAN JOSE

Peck is thinking of emigrating. I must help him more. The orchard case has come to a compromise but it is not absolutely settled yet. I have left my bond wherein I agree to deliver up the orchard on the 1st of October. My lawyer will not give it to the bishop until the bishop gives him a paper. Must be as guarded as ever.

Wheat has failed severely in Soquel and Peck is near destroyed. There are general complaints all over the Country. He is next to try raising stock. I do not see how he can fail at that, too. Henry is capable of finding the most different and laughable roads to failure.

Fortunes may slip through a man's fingers in this Country very strangely. It's the hardest times now in San Francisco I ever saw. This depression is on us in a rage. Property has no fixed value. I think I am as safe in my loans as any man in the City but there is no telling when I may slip up on some of my loans. I will be as cautious as man can be, in fact, I have sort of looked for just such times as we now have but not quite so soon. Mr. Beard is broke flat, he's not worth a dollar. He was worth $200,000 last year but he speculated a great deal.

I am busy fencing in some more land adjoining the place I bought. Carmel seems quite well. She is able to accept the loss of our beloved children better than I. Her great faith in God helps a great deal. She believes they go directly to heaven to become little angels, dressed all in white. It can even be an occasion of joy. How I long for my little darlings beside me.

9TH JULY 1854

The negotiations for a compromise on the orchard are over. It ended and now I don't intend that those rascally priests shall ever get the orchard by any act of mine. They think to scare me but they are mistaken. Have sent all of Henry Peck's notes to him marked 'paid.' I wish to do him this service for he is a good man and a true friend. Will try to get him a start with pears. There is no part of California so good for fruit as Santa Cruz. He can get a division of the ranch this fall if he and one or two others tries. I am going to set out a fine lot of trees this winter here and also strawberries. There is some in this Valley have made thousands by strawberries this summer. There are not many orchards set out owing to the unsettled state of land titles.

20TH JULY 1854   SAN FRANCISCO, RAPHETTA HOUSE

Time don't make me feel much better in mind. It takes an effort for me to put my mind to business. O, to be afflicted like me. At times I feel as though life was worthless but even though I say this I still . . .

The news from Detroit is another blow. My friend says he heard that my mother is dead, but is not certain. He will send a man to London to enquire. I am confident from the way he wrote that my mother's dead, but he did not like to say so. How few my loved ones grow.

28TH AUGUST 1854   SAN JOSE

A schooner has arrived in San Francisco on Friday with 40 boxes of pears for Peck. I will ship 20 next week. Ricardo and his wife and Elena and Refugio were here to visit.*

More suits in San Francisco. Damn, will they ever get tired of suing after a while.

---

* Friends of Carmel Fallon and other Castro relatives from Santa Cruz.

22ND JANUARY 1855

All is well in San Jose. My business prospers and Carmel is in good health. I have decided to take the formal naturalization steps to become a citizen later this month in San Francisco. I have served this country under arms but still I must swear allegiance in a ceremony. It is a very confusing system.

Have ordered lumber from the mill in Soquel and Peck will pile it up on the prairie as we can get it hauled in May or June cheap. I will send him money to pay Bates for the hauling.

I intend to get a patent from the land office on the first of February. If Tracy would send me those warrants as soon as possible I would not hesitate a moment to write all over the back of them anything Mr. Tracy wants. There is no respect in this world of writing. This damn land business has everyone in a great uproar and panic.

20TH APRIL 1855

Cast my vote today in the election. There were over 400 voters in that day. We are becoming a major city and perhaps can get the Capital returned next year. A man of the Know-Nothings was elected Superintendant of Schools — a strange turn. This party is neither Democrat or Whig but is against both. They are against Catholics, Mexicans, emigrants, and a host of other groups. They make me quite nervous. I don't like people who only know what they are against not what they are for. And now a man who glories in knowing nothing is to teach young children to know <u>something</u>. I fear for our city.

> Ed.: *In the State election of the Fall, 1855, Fallon's fears were confirmed when a virulently Nativist candidate was elected to be Governor. The major plank of this candidate was opposition to all things not white, Anglo-Saxon, or Protestant.*

22ND MAY 1855

Again clouds are on the horizon. A vigilante group is organized in San Francisco to restore order. We had a meeting to vote support. Ex-Governor, I like the sound of 'ex', Peter Burnett, spoke against the motion. This appeared to seal its success and it passed with only a few gainsayers.

23RD JUNE 1855

Sent by a safe conveyance the mortgage of Scott and copy of the note to Peckham. Have told him to sue on and foreclose the same. This is the customary way as a lawyer's office is unsafe for notes. I feel a little like a landlord in Ireland with the foreclosing business but I must protect my property.

14TH JULY 1855

Today I have finished a venture that will be of great importance to my fortune. I purchased a beautiful piece of property of 100 varas square from William Daniels. It is north of Santa Clara Street on San Pedro in the luxuriant mustard fields that flow down to the Guadalupe. My neighbors are the Peralta girls, daughters of Don Luis, and the Chaboyas whose property is north of mine. The sisters of Notre Dame convent and school grounds back on to my land. The old *acequia* area is a beautiful place. This is rich land for growing. Pellier has many fine trees in his orchard down San Pedro Street. Some cuttings he has imported from France and Spain. When I walk down to the River I am reminded very much of London and my youth. Almost I feel the hand of John Jennings on my shoulder. But one can't go back. I am here now.

15TH JULY 1855

Father Goetz baptized my new daughter Ana this morning at St. Joseph's. A good Jesuit it appears. *Patrinos* were Miguel Felis and Dominga Higuera. Many of the relatives were over from Santa Cruz and Soquel. Peck and Antonia, Josefa, Guadalupe, the others, but not the old woman. Judge Blackburn was very taken with wine at the ceremony, as was Peckham. My old enemy of '46, Dolores Pacheco was very happy at the ceremony. He praised me as a man of great resolve and courage. I began to think much more of Pacheco's judgement from that moment. Antonio Pico, patron of the Church and Daniels were also there. My new life is now truly begun.

13TH NOVEMBER 1855

A happy summer. Plans were well begun for our new home. Then the lawyers and suits begin anew. I sick to heart with them. Jesuits. Old Bates did not want to pay the lumber. Peckham said he intended to charge me fifty dollars in case Bates stood to the argument but since Bates backed out he would not charge anything until the suit was decided. I will not be humbugged by Bates and I will not lessen the rent one jot. The more you give in, the more he wants. Peckham is continuing the suit with the Jesuits. I do not know whether the Upper Ranch will be confirmed in the other courts for now there will be strong opposition.

Pears and strawberries are more to my liking. I raised a pear this year that weights a pound and nine ounces and it's of the first quality Come December the crop will be ripe.

21st NOVEMBER 1855

Have written to Peck to find a person to haul the lumber from Soquel to San Jose next Spring. I can get it done for twelve or fifteen dollars a thousand and I think it will be very dry and light. A team can haul two thousand feet at a twin load. The finest wood for the finest home in San Jose.

2nd MARCH 1856

When I receive the post from Santa Cruz I always gird for bad news. The Church has become heir to the 1/9 of the Rancho which the old woman possessed — some type of bequest. It was surely not one at her death bed for she is as full of vigor and treachery as ever. She travels about the land like a hag of old, spreading problems. Of late she has taken to dragging her new husband, the Frenchman, Louis Depeau along with her.

17th MARCH 1856

Met with Adolf Pfister, Pomeroy and others of the Democrat Party at United States Hotel on San Pedro. We are all anxious to clear up the problems of our city. A gambling element is quite active at the French Hotel on Market and Eldorado.* The men wish me to stand for Election to the Board of Trustees. I wish to help and participate but am quite torn.

16th APRIL 1856

This day I have stood and been elected to the Board of Trustees of San Jose, We are five. It is merely the *Ayutamiento* and *alcalde* of the old days, except with less power. A radical change should be made in our form of government. C. W. Pomeroy and Levi Goodrich serve with me.

* Coincidentally, at the time of this writing, 1978, it is still the site of a card club at Post Street (Eldorado) which the San Jose Police Department has recently suspended for licensing violations. History repeats itself.

17TH JUNE 1856

Most of the local men have forwarded a letter to the Vigilantes of San Francisco, endorsing their actions. There are six thousand of them and they have cannons. Men are ordered out of the City, many Irish and Democrats. All friends of Senator Broderick. I fear they are a pack of rabble and will have no truck or dealings with these vigilantes.

19TH AUGUST 1856

A bitter election campaign is being fought this year for President. My old comrade John Charles Fremont is the candidate of the new Republican Party. I did not think he had much of a chance but never should he be taken lightly. With pretty Jessie to help him, he will do a good job for the New Republicans. I do not think I can vote for him.

28TH OCTOBER 1856

The campaign has taken a dirty turn. The Know Nothing group loudly condemns Fremont for being a Catholic and worse. He is no Catholic, I know this for sure. Old Tom Benton has taken the side of James Buchanan, the Democrat. A cruel blow. It is certain that this county will vote Democrat. They are all in a panic about the nigger-lovers, radicals, prohibitionists, free-lovers and others who make up the Republican Party. A pack of fools and blackguards spreading such falsehoods. Again I say that Know Nothing is a good name for the bastards.

1ST NOVEMBER 1856

Torch light rally on St. James Square. More here than at the old bear and bull fights. Nearly had to strike a blow against a foul-mouthed fellow who spoke about the "strange" birth* of Fremont and also made a comment about Jessie. Perhaps he thought that it was permissable since I was a Democrat. I am first a comrade of Fremont. Pfister prevailed on me to leave the man alone.

Heard on a broadside sheet a rhyme about John C. that went "Arise, arise, ye braves, and let our war cry be, Free Speech, Free Press, Free Soil, Free Men, Fre-mont and Victory!" Good, but I fear to no avail for my old friend. The Pathfinder is how they call him now. That is a name Tom Fitzpatrick would laugh to hear.

---

* The fact Fremont was illegitimate was raised by the opposition in the 1856 election with much damage. It was a dirty, rough campaign even for those days.

Market Street in San Jose, 1859

The Fallon House, c. 1868. On the left is the Peralta Adobe.

20TH NOVEMBER 1856

The election is over. Fremont piled up many votes, over a million, but the South and President Fillmore's Know Nothings took a heavy toll. Buchanan is elected. In our county John was defeated 576 to 809 for Buchanan. I am sorry.

3RD JANUARY 1857

The year begins in a very prosperous manner. The pears off the fifteen trees in my orchard have been sold for $800.00. A handsome profit for such a short time venture. All the trees are in fine shape. Between the Pelliers and myself this is the center of a fine fruit area.

> Ed.: *The Pellier mentioned here is Louis, a French orchardist who introduced the "petit d'agen" prune at his City Gardens nearby and began the preeminance of the Santa Clara Valley in that field. In the next century, the Valley would have one-third of the total prune acreage in the world.*

2ND FEBRUARY 1857

A earthquake has destroyed much of the mission in Santa Cruz, Peck writes me. No one hurt but perhaps there is a god watching us. The priests have been confirmed in the mission for years and now it crumbles. The orchard case is lost to us I fear. Peck has not been able to manage it. He is not able to collect from Bates any of the rent owed even though Bates has just completed a steam mill on the river. Lumber will sell for $35 a thousand and still no money to us. I shall have to handle this myself.

My errant brother-in-law is too good natured. He dreams now of a quartz mine on the upper ranch. Fremont and Godey tried that game on the Mariposa Rancho and have yet to pay for all the equipment purchased. It is a bad business.

17TH MAY 1857

Another addition to our family. Carmel is well and we have a daughter Emma. Antonio Pico and Pilar Bernal will stand as *comadre* and *copadre* this next month. Work on the Board of Trustees takes a good deal of my efforts. I miss the work at my own orchard.

The Fallon House in 1876

The Fallon House at the turn of the century with the new western addition.

30TH MARCH 1858

The business of San Jose keeps me from my business. I will not be a candidate at the next election. The beautiful home on San Pedro Street is done and there are few that can equal it in the area. Carmel is very proud. It is two high stories with a ten foot foundation to save us from the yearly floods. Marble fireplaces are in most of the rooms. It is wonderful.

Judge Watson asked to borrow some money to locate school land warrants on some redwoods near the line of the road from here to Santa Cruz. I would not let him have any.

27TH APRIL 1858   NEW YORK

Arrived by sea after a pleasant trip. Today it snowed.

20TH MAY 1858   NEW YORK

It has rained for all but a few days. Except for a few fine days. I don't like the climate here at all. Indeed no Californian can enjoy himself here. I found my brother's children well and left my niece at the school where she was and the little boy also. I will leave them there for two years. I went west only as far as Siracuse and south as far as Washington and northeast in Connecticut. Tired of traveling in cars. Didn't go to Michigan and was on the next train to the smashup on the Central road where so many were killed.

1ST JULY 1858   SAN JOSE

Home. All my family here is in first rate health and my gardens flourishing. I will have a full crop of pears but no peaches or apricots.

13TH OCTOBER 1858

Purchased a bit of land from Colonel Naglee, the officer who came to California with Stevenson's New York Volunteers. It is a beautiful little *vega*. Wanted to talk politics all morning. Fremont, Gwin, just about anyone at all. When he began to ramble about the price of plots at the Oak Hill Cemetery, I took my leave.

Ed.: Fallon was listed as grantee or purchaser of many parcels over the next few years; he acquired the following: 18 Dec. 1857, J-336, J. H. Scull. 8 Feb. 1859, M-177, Antonio Chaboya. 25 May 1859, M-133, Joseph Aram, 1 Aug. 1859, M-472, J. H. Moore. 30 Jan. 1860, N-74, R. G. Moody. 1 Feb. 1860, N-81, Lightston. 24 May 1861, O-301 J. Parr. 28 May 1861, O-302, N. Mathers. 6 June 1863, R-195, M. Wise. He was as noted, also active in Santa Cruz County property through these same years. The 1876 Thompson and West Historical Atlas will list him with 5000 acres, second largest ownership in Santa Clara County.

16TH MARCH 1859

Once again my time is not my own. An Act to incorporate the City of San Jose has been passed and the government will be vested in a Mayor, a Common Council of five members, a City Marshall and City Assessor. I will stand for Mayor.

29TH MARCH 1859

I don't know whether to rejoice or sorrow. I have been elected Mayor. Pomeroy, Moody and Adolf Pfister are also elected to the Council. We may once and for all clear up the questions of land title and restore confidence and order to our land. These things I have vowed to do and I shall.

The complete text of a speech delivered by His Honor, Mayor Fallon, to the Common Council:

To the matter of the lands of the pueblo or city of San Jose, I will call your particular attention. There is no question which can come before you during your term of office, that demands so much of your attention as this; and it is hoped that in all matters affecting land titles, you will act with caution and be guided by justice, always having in view the settlement of titles in such a manner as will perfect the same. Not the amount of money to be derived, but the quieting of titles should be the main aim. Nothing tends so much to the prosperity of a community as the certainty of titles to the homes they occupy. Improvements are then made of a permanent nature, which add to the general wealth, and, as a consequence, increase the public revenue; besides, it makes people feel attached to their homes, and will induce many to live here permanently, who would otherwise leave the place, and perhaps the State. The sooner titles to land are settled, the better; for the longer it is delayed the more complicated will it get. Fortunately for this pueblo, the titles have not got in such a snarl but that it can be unraveled; but to do so, and make perfect deeds, it will be necessary that there be a unanimity of action by all the parties in authority, as well as some who have judgement liens on the pueblo lands. Of these I will briefly give you a history:

This pueblo was established in the year 1777, and was endowed with a large domain. The least quantity granted to any pueblo was four square leagues of land; but some pueblos had more, and this being one of the most important in the State, is believed to have had many more leagues than the pueblos of lesser note. The titles of the pueblos are the oldest, for no title was given to individuals until several years after the establishment of pueblos. The King of Spain and the Governors of California were always careful to make inquiry in regard to grants to individuals, and to know that such grants did not encroach upon the lands of the pueblo. The authorities of the pueblos had power to make grants of land, either for building or agricultural purposes. All the lands remaining unoccupied by any particular individual, was used in common for all grazing purposes.

The authorities of the city, at present, have all the powers in regard to the disposal of lands that the former authorities ever had, for the Legislature in granting us a charter, could not take away any of our rights as a pueblo, nor does it attempt to do so, but gives us additional powers in regard to municipal regulations within certain limits. The Supreme Court of ths State has given the opinion in several cases, holding good titles derived from the authorities of pueblos, both before and after the occupancy of this country by the Americans.

In 1847 Burton was *Alcalde*, and called a meeting (or junta) of the heads of families, in regard to the commons. It was then decided that the commons should be surveyed into five-hundred-acre lots, and that there should be only so much of the pueblo lands surveyed as would give the head of each family five hundred acres, and, in order that the division should be fair, it was decided to place the numbers of the lots in a hat; one to be drawn by each person as his name was called; and the number so drawn to his name, to be his five-hundred-acre lot; and he to have a lease of the same for ninety-nine years.

The first judgement lien, in all the lands of the pueblo, was created by endeavoring to provide suitable accommodation for the Legislature. In the formation of our State Constitution, the capital was located at San Jose, and most of the prominent men who then resided here, in order to keep the capital at this place, advanced money to the city and loaned their credit, so that the city might be able to pay rents of offices and houses, as well as to purchase the building occupied by the Legislature. Thus was our first debt created which never has been finally satisfied. The Legislature at length removed the capital, and left us our debts; but they allowed us a small sum — fifty thousand dollars in scrip, which sold for forty cents on the dollar — which sum fell short, by several thousand dollars, of paying the debt created. Interest was then very high, from the fact that money was worth a great deal for investment, as lands were low; and, in order to stop interest, both the city and her creditors were willing to arrange the matter satisfactorily (as will fully appear by reference to proceedings of City Council in 1850-51). All the lands of the pueblo were sold at Sheriff's sale and bid in by the creditors, and then they entered into an agreement, with the Mayor and Council, that two of their number and the Mayor should have power to convey the interest of all the parties concerned. This is the condition of the first judgment lien at present.

The second judgement lien was created in 1854. The Supreme Court decided that San Jose was the legal capital, and they made it the capital, in fact, for they came here and held their court, and the people were assured by some of the Judges that the Legislature would have to meet here. So again the people were called on to provide accommodation for the Legislature — the first Capitol building having been destroyed by fire. An election was held, and it was decided to erect a suitable building. Accordingly our present City Hall was built, and a debt of forty-eight thousand dollars created thereby. In the meantime one of the Judges died and another was appointed in his place. The Court then reversed the former opinion, and decided that San Jose was not the capital. So that, between the Legislature and the Supreme Court, our city has been made to pay rather too dear for the floating Capitol.

However, in order to get rid of the high rate of interest accumulating on the money borrowed, a Funding Bill was passed, and the debt funded; and for the purpose of securing to the creditors the sure payment thereof, three Fund Commissioners were created, whose duty it is to sell the property of the city, with consent of the city authorities, and to pay all the proceeds into the treasury for the liquidation of said debt. This is the condition, at present, of the second judgement lien on the pueblo lands.

In order to make a good title, free and clear from all judgments or any cloud whatever, it will be necessary:

First, For the trustees of the first judgment, composed of the Mayor and two of the judgment creditors, to make a deed. I will here state that I have conversed with both of the gentlemen representing the creditors, upon this subject, and I am led to believe that they will make deeds of their interest for a mere nominal sum. They also assure me that they have power of attorney to sell, from all the parties interested. And for my part, as trustee from the city by virtue of my office, if I had the power, I would make good all deeds to the citizens without charge; and I think the city would then be the gainer; but as there are debts to pay, as a matter of justice, the parties benefited ought to pay something, so that our liabilities may be met, and justice done to all.

Second, A deed from the Fund Commissioners, sanctioned by the city authorities, will, in addition to the first, be a good title of all the interest of the pueblo, and, I think, as good as any title in the State.

Care should be taken by you to have the whole business in this matter legally done. I would recommend that you take it in hand immediately, and have some of your Body appointed to confer with the trustees of the first judgment, and Fund Commissioners, so that you may all act in amity.

Ed.: *Fallon had obviously learned a good deal of law in his forays to court and grasped both the problem and the fact that a speedy solution was absolutely imperative to the well-being of the community. The first Legislature, that of the many drinks, had met in San Jose in January of 1849. By the Second Legislature in January of 1852, Vallejo and the anti-San Jose Group had accomblished their goal and the "fait accompli" of February was academic: the Capital was removed. Although ordered back to San Jose by a Supreme Court decision in March, 1854, it was simply not to be. The suits resulting from the indebted pueblo lands, the famous "Forty Thieves Title," involved James Frazier Reed, Josiah Belden, Naglee and other prominent community leaders. Litigation continued unabated until 1869 when in* Braham et al vs. City of San Jose, *the Supreme Court ruled "that city lands were not subject to execution and sale by judgement," hence the judgement and sheriff's sale were voided. So came to an end the ignominious tale of San Jose, the State Capital.*

Andres Pico, commander of the Californio forces at San Pascual and later State Senator.

30TH MARCH 1859

This city is still reeling over the murders on San Fernando Street. A trial was proceeding in the 3rd District Court of Judge Sam Bell McKee. The men were shot down outside near noon time. Crosby was being tried for murder and C. T. Ryland, Burnett's son-in-law, was defending him. Crosby was shot dead with one bullet in the head. One bystander was also killed. With Ryland as his attorney, defending him, I say that someone just removed the middleman.

11TH APRIL 1859

A very serious meeting was held in Evergreen in regard to the Chaboya title on the Rancho Yerba Buena or Socayre. There are many settlers and squatters in this area and severe trouble may result if the title is not soon quieted. This is another granted by Figueroa to Don Antonio in the same year as Soquel.

12TH MAY 1859

Money expended by the city last year was $11,768.80, including the redemption of bonds. We give too much for frivolous things and must contain ourselves.

1ST JULY 1859

The fund debt is $1800.00. I have given public notice that the City has no interest in selling its 500 acres. The actions of the San Jose Land Company is beyond belief.

24TH AUGUST 1859

Horace Greeley the New York newspaper man spoke here. Met him briefly and was quite impressed. My last official act as Mayor. I am through with politics for good perhaps.

3RD SEPTEMBER 1859

Andres Pico paid his respects today. Traveling through to Sacramento and the old lancer is at it again. He will introduce a bill in the Legislature to split the state of California in half. Those in the north can't check lawlessness and protect them against the Indians, he says. I think Don Andres wants to be Governor. He had his chance to split the state at San Pascual and failed. It was a good try though. He seems very fit and inquires about old enemies — Carson and Fremont.

29TH OCTOBER 1859

Fires to the east. John Brown of the Osawtomie massacre has seized Harpers Ferry in Virginia. After much gun play he was captured and executed. The slavery and abolitionist factions are more excited than ever. I fear that this trouble will spread over the land, even to our lovely valley.

29TH JULY 1860

Aiken was here today. He had been out in the mountains towards Livermore's ranch and brought in a number of specimens of rock. Said he had discovered a quicksilver mine. He has faith in it and left mysteriously early tonight. He has made a claim for Peck and I. Would like him to go to the Coso mines discovered east of Visalia to stake a claim. Peck is very excited about the prospect of our silver mine.

LETTER TO HENRY PECK, 21st AUGUST, 1860

Dear Henry,

I had an assay made of the rock from our silver mine and you may depend it was a thorough assay and correct and what do you think was the result — why . . . don't get excited but this must be told. Keep your shirt on while you read the result, don't whoop and holler. Well here it is — there is not one darned cent of silver or gold in it — it is chiefly black oxide of manganeze and iron. But perhaps you had better say nothing about it, so that Aiken when he comes up may sell to the others for something —

We are all well; hoping you and family are.

I remain as Ever

Yours Truly,
Thomas Fallon

21ST AUGUST 1860

The great gold rush of 1860 is over. It ended in an assay report this morning. Such is life.

1st OCTOBER 1860

There is much talk of the coming election and what will follow it. Our union is held together by a thin thread. The Republicans have put up Abraham Lincoln and the Democrats are split between Douglas and Breckenridge. If any of the southern states leave the Union, I fear the seccessionists in this county will start to talk about California leaving. Some rumors say that if California does not leave then Santa Clara County will secede from California.

7th NOVEMBER 1860

Lincoln has received the most votes of the four candidates and will be our President. In Santa Clara County he got 1447, Douglas the Northern Democrat, 881, and Breckenridge received 722. War will now surely come.

20th APRIL 1861

Lincoln cannot stop the drift to complete and total war. The southern states are out of the Union. Here we fare little better. The Chaboya Grant was confirmed for Yerba Buena, and a large posse failed to respond to Marshall Gunn's commands. It will be a settlers war as I have long feared. Several hundred of them paraded through town with a small cannon. The Commission waited so long to patent this land that poor fellows have made great improvements to their land which they now do not own. We are being true to Commodore Sloat's Proclamation, to guarantee property and protect title, but I don't think Leroy and their families feel any better.

22nd JULY 1861

A great battle has been fought in Virginia. It is at Manassas Junction. Many have died. The Union, I believe, will soon be torn asunder with no hope of reconciliation.

15th MARCH 1862

Smallpox in San Jose. Many of the poorer people have died. Thank God all four of my children escaped its ravages.

1st APRIL 1862

They will open Reed to Almaden Street. Three schooners a week leave from Alviso to San Francisco. It could be a great port one day.

4TH APRIL 1862

The new editor of the paper, a J. J. Owen, writes with a good touch. He supported my opponent Senator Wallis but I have to applaud when he says that California has 868 lawyers, that is a big load for a 12 year old state to shoulder.* He has also petitioned the Common Council to exterminate all dogs which he believes comprise about fifty tons in this city, saying a pack nearly trampled him in Washington Square.

7TH APRIL 1862

The news weighs heavy on all of us. A great battle has been fought at Shiloh. Twenty thousand are dead including General Albert Sidney Johnson who I knew in California. I don't believe that I am ready to live in a world where so much slaughter is the way of things. The bodies piled as high as on the Kinsale ditch are at Shiloh, too. I long for the uncivilized days, the days of Jim Bridger and his coat of armour warding off Indian lances, the Cheyenne with their *coup* sticks, and the land of the Californios. Much fun is poked at Castro and Alvarado but when you think of the *pronunciamentos* and *manifestos*, the war of words, is it not better? When Castro paraded before Fremont at Gavilan Peak is it not preferable to this wholesale bloody butchery. I harken back to those days with joy. I do not wish to record more of this insanity. For a time only my family and my orchard will be my interest.

✤   ✤   ✤

10TH APRIL 1865

I will write that yesterday the major Confederate Armies surrendered at Appomattox in Virginia. We will see how Lincoln can manage the peace.

---

*In 1862, Fallon was defeated for State Senator by Mr. Wallis, a resident of Mayfield, present day Palo Alto. The editor of the San Jose Mercury, J. J. Owen, was a brash, opinionated man and occasional opponent of Fallon on municipal policies. Owen's crowning achievement was the erection of the Great Light Tower.

General Fremont as he looked during the Civil War and shortly before the southern rendezvous with Fallon.

11TH APRIL 1865

Two days in a row. It must be like a disease. Someone said that Jasper Gunn, our City Marshall who absconded with $2763.48 has been seen in Mexico. I remember when Ramon Romero was hung for grand larceny in November of 1862. Stole $43. I guess it is all a matter of being in the right place — in Jaspar's case, Mexico. He was the loudest to condemn when the Government introduced paper money due to war problems in 1862. It must have been a hell of a lot lighter for him.

Soon the famous San Jose Volunteers and the New Almaden Calvary will return. Instead of chasing Indians in Arizona they could have chased the Confederates in this county who have been stealing horses and chickens "for Jeff Davis."

Heard of two acquaintances — Isaac Graham died last year in Santa Cruz. My mourning period will be brief. General Naglee is coming home after his efforts in the war. John C. Fremont has still not forgiven Lincoln for relieving him of his command in Missouri during the early days of the war. It is said he is heading home to the Mariposa Ranch.

19TH APRIL 1865

Received a letter from John C. Fremont. I am to travel south and meet Alex Godey. This is to be a very interesting trip.

> Ed.: *Here was the area where a long, almost diary-like entry is made of the strange events of the next eighteen months. As I noted in my introduction, this is a very interesting and historically worthwhile tract, but largely outside the scope and tenor of this* Journal.

1ST MARCH 1867

The new year has been full of events for me since my return from the south. All is well in San Jose and the beautiful part of the Rancho Soquel which last year was bought for us is the finest of the entire Grant.* The high plateau with the fertile soil and fine vegetation has long been a favorite place of mine and I feel the best in the whole vicinity.

---

* In Fallon's absence, a 2/27 share of the Soquel Rancho was purchased from Richard Hyde for $3000.00. It was the high, eastern bluff area above the present downtown of Capitola and running to the boundary of Aptos Rancho. It was finalized on 20 April, 1866.

Protest against extending Montgomery Street to be presented on the 11th of March, 1867. Marked "Draft."

To the Honorable President and Board of Supervisors of the City and County of San Francisco.

Gentlemen:

In the matter of opening and extending Montgomery Street from Market to Chassel. Your Petitioners attention is called to your resolution No. 6370 when in it is proposed to assess my lot for supposed benefits. The said lot is 34 feet 4½ inches on Montgomery Street by sixty feet on Sutter Northwest Corner and 75 x 75 feet on the Third and Mission Northwest Corner. Your Petitioner will beg leave most respectfully to enter my earnest protest against any assessment for the extending of Montgomery Street because I believe it would lower the value and profits of the lots on Third and Montgomery Street — as well as many other streets. Market and Licona would be lowered in value. I believe the City would not be any gainer but the reverse, a loser, for what you might get from the extension of Montgomery you would more than lose by the depreciation of property on other streets. I don't think it right that I should be made to pay for the improving of other people's property for clearly this move of extending Montgomery Street must be a speculation of those who own property in the middle of the blocks that the street would go through. Then if they want a street, let them pay for it like all the new streets heretofore opened. I have thus stated candidly to your Honorable Body some of my views believing your intention to do justice to all your constituents and taxpayers to the best of your judgement. I will only add that all the persons that I have spoken to most clearly interested in the welfare of the city at large and particularly the owners of property and taxpayers on Montgomery and Third Streets are all opposed to the extending of Montgomery Street, much less to be taxed for it — for it is their opinion and mine that we have ample outlets now to South of Market Street and the proposed extension would cut the property that it passes through at such an angle as would make most or either side in a very bad shape. Many would have but very little depth there by preventing the street from being opened on and would make the crossing of Third and all South of it a bad and dangerous condition for pedestrians.

Trusting this protest will meet your favorable consideration.

I have the honor to be your obedient servant.

Thomas Fallon

Ed.: The above is a very interesting piece of work. It shows a clear grasp of local politics, land values, and urban planning, with a smattering of simple traffic control thrown in for good measure. A balance between accusing the Board of being fools or worse and the pose of a humble supplicant is quite an act of artistry: Thomas Fallon seems to have done it. Charles Clayton, Esquire, former Alcalde of Santa Clara, made the presentation in Fallon's stead. About this year Montgomery was a fashionable promenade, lined with elegant shops; shortly after this, Kearny superseded it as the preferred street. The effect of this particular cut through is difficult to ascertain.

3RD APRIL 1867

Much against my better judgement, friends have prevailed on me to run for county treasurer.

26TH APRIL 1867

Attended the dedication of the new, magnificent Courthouse on St. James Square last week. It is a beautiful building and Goodrich should be greatly praised. I told him that he probably would be so praised after he was dead. He stared at me queerly. If that had been standing in 1852 we would still have the capital here.

27TH APRIL 1867

Moody has been defeated for the treasurers post. My victory was by 61 votes. I believe I am the lucky one.

30TH JUNE 1867

It is necessary to record this month that the Emperor Maximillian of the Hapsburg family was executed in Mexico. If only he had been able to listen to the least whit of reason he might have saved himself. Not a bad man for a nobleman of high rank. Alex Godey liked him greatly.*

MARCH 1868

Railroad Franchise given by Legislature for a local San Jose line. Do not believe it will be successful.

---

* At this point in time the physical characteristics of Fallon have come down to us in the invaluable interview conducted with one Fanny Montgomery by the indefatigable Clyde Arbuckle. She describes Fallon as "somewhat Mark Twainish in appearance, with a fine well-formed face. He reportedly glittered when he walked and doffed his hat with a cavalier flourish to ladies he would meet, revealing a great shock of hair."

JOAQUIN MURIETA

An original drawing by Charles Nahl, San Francisco 1859.

Joaquin Murieta, "Fremont's boy."

21st OCTOBER 1868

Most severe earthquake ever in San Jose. My home is fine but the Peralta's adobe is badly cracked. Many other buildings are down.

10th November 1868

Wars make Presidents. General Grant has soundly defeated his opponent. Santa Clara County went closely to the General. No more.

25th December 1868

Many have died this year. Majors is dead in Santa Cruz. Captain Love, the man who killed Joaquin Murieta, was himself shot by his hired man. Always believed he shot the Mexican while asleep. Fremont's boy.* The Cooper man was set to get a wife, the daughter of Dubois, and instead received two barrels of a shotgun when he walked up the porch stairs. Things are quiet in this part of the city. Much disarray elsewhere.

18th MAY 1869

The Central Pacific and the Union Pacific have been joined in Utah at Promontory Point. This nation is one. Soon it will be possible to ride from San Francisco to New York. Impossible to fathom. The changes are so rapid. Surely it was not that long ago that we came to the peak and saw the valley of the Sacramento smiling before us — surely not so far removed.

3rd NOVEMBER 1869

The newspaper this day carried some cheerful happening. It said that on "Saturday evening ex-Governor Peter Burnett was run over in consequence of the rapid and careless driving of an unknown person on Third Street." Could be it was the result of Burnett's careless and rapid land speculation in Alviso. Saw J. J. Owen at the Richeleau Theatre and he said he almost printed the belief that poor Burnett could well be lying on Third Street yet if only those who knew him passed by. Fortunately for the ex-Governor, a man from Santa Cruz who did not know his face or history gave him succor.

---

* John Fremont encountered a young Mexican orphan on his second expedition, named Pablo. Godey and Carson revenged the death of the boy's father and he was taken to the home of Senator Benton. Fremont always maintained, according to the premiere authority, Allan Nevins in <u>Fremont, Pathmarker of the West,</u> that the boy escaped and became the Robin Hood bandit, Joaquin Murietta.

Christopher "Kit" Carson

12TH DECEMBER 1869

The Common Council has finally begun to make some improvements to the St. James Square Park. It is a municipal disgrace, when most of the streets are guttered, graded, curbed, and with open sewers, though not as good as in some places. We now have 8 churches and a population of 9,118 in the confines of the city. So changed.

31ST DECEMBER 1869

I now close the year of 1869 with the thoughts of never perhaps opening this book again. There are fewer and fewer things which I care to record and I often wonder if it would not be best to discard it as I have so many memories. Over half a century I have lived and much has been my pain and sorrow. All in the way of pleasures I have — my home, my wife and new family, beautiful trees. All that a man should have to be the constant envy of all. Yet — many of my old comrades have died or will soon. Carson is gone in the fall of this year. Fremont is reported ill. Godey has fallen from sight. Maxwell is said to have died in New Mexico. All gone and none to replace them in my affections.

I think of my little darlings in New Orleans and curse the day I saw that black harbor. If only I could do it once again.

V

The Return

15TH NOVEMBER 1875

THE BEGINNING again to record in this journal is not an easy
task after so long a respite. Perhaps it's my old comrade Blackburn that makes me write today. How happy he was. With a fortune in
potatoes and land, well respected, a fine wife and baby son. Then all
crumbled. The child died and Blackburn died a few years later with no
desire to go on. Many times I would attempt to lift his spirits but he
was so weary. The laughing face when we rode south with Fremont
and the Battalion had no more laughter in it. Pfister read to me a piece
of Greek tragedy that I remember well. Judge no man happy, they say,
until he is dead. So much intervenes. My oldest daughter is married.
Carmel still writes to the old woman and sees her when we go to the
Soquel. I will never speak to that harridan.

There is a spirit of unrest and dissatisfaction abroad in the country. No more boom times and easy money. No bonanzas. Capital is
now scarce and interest prohibitive. Many thousands move to the cities
to get relief. Poverty and unemployment are the rule. Capitalists are
shunned and there is great animosity against men of prosperity. Grant
and his Whiskey Ring rob us at one level while the local people charge
us for streets we do not want.*

They are poltroons of a high order. Our Legislature is little better. The *Bulletin* of San Francisco recently congratulated the people
of the state for our legislators, saying even though evincing ignorance
and incapacity, they seemed to be more influenced by political pre-
judice and personal ambititon than mercenary motives. This only means
that the Railroads are not paying enough graft this session. They will
rectify it next one. While the State falls ino ruin they can discuss the

---

* The extension of San Augustine Street (now St. John Street) was put through west of San
Pedro Street, between Fallon's home and the Peralta Adobe; it apparently assessed him
money. The Whiskey Ring along with the "Credit Mobilier" were two of the more famous
exposes of the scandal-ridden Grant Administration.

problem of the 'celestial coolie' — out with the Chinese! There are any number of people I would rather have out than those poor souls.

San Jose has a water company that charges us to drink. McLaughlin and Rankin help run it. Four years ago the College of Notre Dame and the entire west end of town was under three feet of water, my home, too. Now they sell water. They have a twenty-five year monopoly to furnish water and get the use of the Los Gatos Creek. We hung Tiburcio Vasquez in the Square for lesser crimes.

3RD MARCH 1876

Took a very long walk. Down to the river and through the old part of town. Stopped for a moment at the site of the *juzgado* where we raised the flag. Was it really thirty years?

17TH MARCH 1876

I had a drink with Adolf Pfister at his store. We discussed the coming elections. I spoke but I care little for the topic.

26TH JUNE 1876

The Santa Clara Street buildings on the corner of San Pedro are very splendid. The Farmers Union has moved there from Pfister's building and is doing very well. Le France has built a building next to it facing the main street. John W. Lyndon from Los Gatos called on me to sell some property. I do not like or trust him but I believe he will persevere until he finds some and becomes a leading citizen of this area. He had Mountain Charlie McKiernan with him, a very likeable sort. I am quite sure that when that grizzly bear ate half of his skull, it was the half with the brain in it. They went over to see the Peralta girl, I fear. The old Don would have handled them quite rapidly. There was a man of good perspective. The land is our gold, go to the ranch, he told his sons. Let the Americans have the golden rocks. How right. I wonder if we would have had bloodshed the day we rode in from Santa Cruz, bold and fearless, if not for Don Luis. *Alcalde* Pacheco listened to him well. Governments change — Spanish, Mexican, American — most things remain the same. I sometimes long for Vallejo and Castro again. The old times are so much more pleasurable from the vantage point of today.

Saw Margaret McBride, the dressmaker, over near Third Street.

Pfister's building and the Farmer's Union

Judge David Belden

7TH DECEMBER 1876

There is no way to repair the damage done. Carmel has fled from the house, taking the four children with her. I don't know how I can reconcile what has happened. The blow to my head was severe. I think she meant to kill me with the iron bar. Once a thing has happened it is so very easy to say how it might have been avoided. I feel lost.

16TH DECEMBER 1876

I did not get to even talk with Carmel at the Court today. Her attorney, Delmas kept her far away like in a cloister and after, spirited her through the St. James Square to a carriage. They accuse me in front of Judge Belden of adultery with Maggie McBride, mental cruelty, physical persecution, and all sorts of blackguardry. This is all too impossible to believe. Our community property is set at $300,000 dollars and Carmel wishes division of same and all the children.

I will not lose my children again. Never will I surrender my family.

17TH December 1876

The records are clear. At the time of our marriage in Santa Cruz my worth was $20,000.00. My lawyer Spencer has all the information. Carmel has a separate worth of $50,000.00 and took $3,000.00 of mine when she left. Our position is quite sound.

I do not wish this thing that is upon me.

4TH JANUARY 1877

All of our property is now conveyed to J. Ellard Bean for reconveyance. The lawyers again have been successful. My will has been thwarted.

3RD FEBRUARY 1877

Judge Belden made the formal decree today. Carmel receives $30,000.00 in gold and the San Francisco property at 3rd and Minnie. All else is confirmed to me as separate property. The children may decide with whom they live. Belle and Arthur look at me so sadly with great questions in their eyes. What am I to do? The court is decided. Carmel too. Once again they have worked their judgement upon me.*

---

* The records of the 20th District Court are quite lengthy in the divorce proceeding, Case 4800. The complaint and response are complete with the exception of two passages expurgated but still discernable, namely, the charges against Fallon of adultery and the counter charge against Carmel of "wilful and malicious" assault with "intent to kill." Both paragraphs have been struck from the official transcript.

22ND APRIL 1877

The beautiful silver domed Cathedral of St. Joseph's is dedicated today. I shall not go. How Pacheco would love to see what has become of his little brick house of worship.

28TH JUNE 1877

At 3:20 p.m. at the First Presbyterian Church, Samantha Steinhoff and I were married. Dr. Brown and Hanlon were there and Reverend Betts did a good job of officiating.

7TH OCTOBER 1877

Carmel and three henchmen from Soquel have attempted to abduct Arthur from Mrs. Heller's custody in Alameda County. She will be made to pay.

Ed.: *For the next months, and continuing through the summer of 1878, Carmel and Thomas Fallon engaged in legal battles over custody of children, stipends for education, and assorted sundry matters which occasioned their appearance in the 20th District Court on at least 9 or 10 occasions.*

3RD JANUARY 1878

A new year cannot change the trouble I have been given. The lawers plague me as in the days of the Jesuits. My Journal is my only consolation for I know not whom to talk to or confide in. The project for the Soquel Rancho — making a Camp San Jose of it are not proceeding well. Hihn had the better location for his Camp Capitola in the old Soquel Landing beach. Instead of schooners they have tents full of city people. My location on the cliff above the water facing Aptos creek is lovely but more remote. More money is needed to properly develop it.

My wife is a source of little comfort to me. She is a young girl and her head is filled with jibberish. Lately I drink a great deal.

7TH JULY 1878

The day is hot indeed. I record once more the anger my new wife causes me. I do not know how long this can continue unabated.

20TH SEPTEMBER 1878

Just returned from a trip to Washington Territory and Victoria, British Columbia. Samantha came with me on the steamer *Dacotah*. It was disaster. All is lost between us.

The Castro Adobe at Rancho Soquel

Rancho Soquel Beach at the time of Fallon's Camp San Jose.

Thomas Fallon and son, Arthur, on tour.

Ed.: It was in October of 1878 that Samantha Fallon's petition for divorce reached Judge Belden's Court. The complaint was the usual list of mental grievances and physical intimidation, along with some wild charges of pistols brandished and threats to kill her if she spoke to another man. His drinking and jealousy were near manic, according to the second Mrs. Fallon. At one point she was forced to walk two miles on a dark beach below Camp San Jose. Shortly thereafter a dissolution was ordered and a few hundred dollars given to the plaintiff.
This Camp San Jose area was renamed New Brighton somewhere in this span of time by Fallon. He had journeyed to the British resort with his young son at some uncertain date. We can see him, regaled in top hat and cane, gazing with fatherly pride at his son from the photograph of M. W. Hall, 80 West Street, Brighton, England.

23RD MAY 1879   SAN FRANCISCO

I come to the City as often now as I used to in the earlier period. It is a place to enjoy and revel in. The hotels are splendid — The Lick House, the Occidental, and Palace Hotel, a most expensive spot. Of, course, the Russ House owned by one of Stevenson's soldiers is my favorite stopping point. Portsmouth Square is where I find the people to talk to or about. Henry George of the Single Tax Movement is there, and although one tax on land would ruin me, I like the Englishman, and think perhaps he does really have a plan. No one will ever know. It is flighty and impossible to get him support. I see Denis Kearney* often, the hero of the South of Market boys. A real firebrand. He shouts for the Chinese to go as if that will really help his Irishman. When the bishop, Alemany, condemned him in a pastoral letter, I read in the Alta California newspaper, I began to see more good in the man. If they are against him, I may be for him.

30TH MAY 1879

Saw Kearney on the street and asked him if when he said we must do a little judicious hanging of capitalists, he meant me. Yes, he says, Tom, we must do it for the good of the workers. He says it with a twinkle in his eyes. I much prefer him to those about me at all times. When he goes to the sandlots, with his cries of "Judge Lynch!" and "Hemp! Hemp!" and shakes his fist at the Nob Hill interests, he is surely right. They built those railroad mansions on the sweat and blood of a thousand, no ten thousand. Fremont and our party gave

---

* Denis Kearney (1847-1907) was a labor agitator born in Ireland. As the leader of a workingman's movement, the so-called "Sand Lot Party," he exercised extraordinary influence in San Francisco and nearly succeeded in capturing important State offices. His platform was anti-Chinese, banks, and politicians; he ended his life as one of the establishment.

Dennis Kearney haranguing the people.

ST. JOSEPH'S CHURCH. SAN JOSE.

St. Joseph's Church shortly after its dedication

some of it. I grow more bitter with each new entry it appears. Perhaps I should join Kearney and blow up the mail docks. A letter to Godey, another . . . I grow more to resemble the old man who dreams of his days of glory. Mine are surely behind.

✻   ✻   ✻

23RD MAY 1880

A great train wreck occurred at Rincon Gorge going to Santa Cruz. Fifteen are killed and 100 injured. At the Auzerais House I tried to tell a man of the famous Mark Twain earthquake on 1st Street. He failed to understand. Am I really that old or is everyone else just very young and very new to our country? Twain spent a week interviewing the earthquake predictor on 1st and Fountain Alley, a Crowley, who owned a saloon there. The man's self-importance was greatly buoyed by all the attention of this out-of-town newspaper man. Then the story was written, and it told of the damn fool in San Jose who shouts earthquake when a pig brushes against his wall. It was a story we thought no one would forget. Again I misjudge things.

1ST JANUARY 1881

I thought of my mentor Sutter this morning. Dead this last year. He liked to be called the "Commander of the Fortress of New Helvitia." The title was none too good for him. A man who fed the hungry, clothed the naked, and comforted the sick. If it's true that Fremont brought the flood of people, old Sutter was there to welcome them just as he did me. That he died broke in a Pennsylvania hotel,* trying to get some of his land back, brings on a great rage in me. He stood a good deal higher than any I have known.

13TH DECEMBER 1881

I now make entries to begin and close a year it seems. At 6:30 this evening I attended the opening of the Electric Light Tower on Market and Santa Clara Street. Such a sight. Nearly 300 feet high, fully illuminated. They threw the switch and all became like day. A Tower of Babel in San Jose. An earthquake will tumble it surely.**
What more will I live to see?

---

* Actually, Sutter died in a Washington D.C. hotel and is buried in Lititz, Pennsylvania.
** In this assumption, Fallon was wrong. The Tower was the brainchild of the peripatetic J. J. Owens, Editor of the Mercury. Four were envisioned to light the entire city. Only one was ever built and it stood on that corner, weathering the Great Quake of 1906, and collapsed one day in 1915. San Jose was far too briefly the "Beacon of the West."

98

The Electric Tower

THE MODERN MESSIAH.

The young actor at the Auzerais House.

10TH MARCH 1882   SAN JOSE

I write only sparingly nowadays. Even letters I scorn. Carmel lives in San Francisco and Santa Cruz. She and the children prosper. Martina has lost another husband it seems. The French puppy Depeau was reported washed overboard on the return voyage from Hawaii with the old woman, who fetches Kanakas for Spreckles.* Her first husband Cota mysteriously disappears, thought shot. My friend Michael Lodge is lost. And now the Frenchman. To lose one husband is a misfortune. To lose two a tragedy. But to lose three seemed to be a case of pure carelessness. Or worse. God knows how many husbands she can misplace.**

29TH MARCH 1882

Had a rather long discourse in the Auzerais House with an actor of strange demeanor. He wore a costume of velvet breeches and ruffled shirt with bright yellow gloves tucked in his coat. This foppish appearance was very much belied by a ready wit and a good knowledge of Dublin. Rich, the railroad man, played a game of chess with the British lad and lost handily much to his consternation. He returned to his corner and considered his lot. The lad is only twenty-eight or thirty years of age. A very sound evening. I will delay for the moment the idea of closing my San Jose home and moving to San Francisco for permanent residence.

> Ed.: *The second interlude of some length occurs here and in it we are able to see a rejuvenated Thomas Fallon involved in a very specific "transaction," one which holds interest of great magnitude, but again is not critical to the completion of his* Journal, *and has to be sufficiently researched and corroborated before making it available for publication. This interlude re-introduces some well-known characters and old friends of Fallon's as well as two new acquaintenances, and will be of serious concern to the total picture of this era in San Jose. It will be made available at some future date.*

---

* Claus Spreckles, millionaire sugar beet manufacturer, had a factory on Soquel Creek and occasionally dealt with the wily Martina as an agent.

** Compare this with the curious next entry. Also in the play "The Importance of Being Ernest," by Oscar Wilde, Lady Bracknell uttered a few lines very similar to these in spirit. See Act I. Wilde, coincidentally was touring the Bay Area this year.

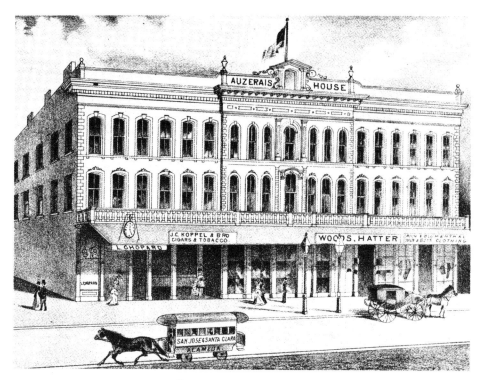

The Auzerais House

San Jose pictured from the Light Tower, 1881, looking north. Market and San Pedro Streets are still dirt and the home of Captain Fallon is visible in the grove of trees.

102

3RD OCTOBER 1884

The spirit in San Jose and indeed all of California is dark. The Chinese are scorned, bullied and berated. This is what civilization is after forty years of our American rule. People are more careful about how they dress or what they say than in what they really are. I wonder how these citizens would regard the motly band of *voyageurs* that rode west with Fremont. Probably they would consider us boorish, maybe even quaint or picturesque. This is my world no longer.

5TH OCTOBER 1884   SAN JOSE

An entry every two or three years seems the best way to continue my writing career. I have no answers to any of the questions that trouble me. My home is very lonely. There are no children about. I miss Carmel. It cannot be right to lose one's family twice. Nine children and none of them with me. I grieve for Thomas Fallon. Is this the end of my life? Do I leave with the lawyers to pick at me and on the breaches that an old man in his kindness and foolishness does?* How better would it be to have never left my native land. It is not right to travel these many long miles and come to this conclusion.

4TH OCTOBER 1885   RUSS HOUSE, SAN FRANCISCO

They tell me I am not well. My kidneys fail me. The pains are severe, but they are not the pain from which I ache. That pain gnaws from even deeper. Where again is my family? Jose Carlos and Maria de los Angeles. Annie and Arthur. Can I have so destroyed the very life blood which first propelled me to this place? Everything is to fade away into nothingness.

Cork, London, Texas, St. Vrain's, Helvitia, Santa Cruz, San Jose, for this small bed and no friendly faces. No voice. Did I kill Xervier and start this journey for this moment?

I will begin again. St. Vrain's can be recovered. It is only a short distance. I can get there soon — the world has been half crossed to arrive at this juncture. Things can be begun anew. I will return.

St. Vrain's

---

* Fallon had been recently sued for breach of promise by a woman named Elmira Dunbar in the 20th District Court at San Jose. A judgement of $10,000.00 was swiftly awarded her by the jury and the case was appealed to the Supreme Court.

The San Jose City Hall as it looked during Fallon's tenure as Mayor in 1859-1860.

Afterword

AS ONE WOULD expect, the life and memory of Captain Thomas Fallon were not easily laid to rest. Controversy swirled about the last years of his life in California. A long and protracted battle in the courts commenced (Fallon must have envisioned this) with Adolf Pfister and two attorneys claiming to have a scribbled will made at the time of death, while his children maintained that the Captain died intestate. Much testimony was taken and the San Francisco and San Jose papers were filled with the conflicting stories and accusations by the contending parties. The estate was said to be vast. Primary among the contentions of his children was the fact that Fallon had "lost his grip" and was constantly intoxicated and often brandished his pistol or sword in a threatening manner. Other more mundane complaints cited by a certain tonsorial artist from Santa Cruz testified to Fallon's great concern with how the hair on the back of his neck was shaved, and his rather extreme use of perfume. All this rhetoric and hypocrisy came to an abrupt end when the Probate Court awarded the bulk of the estate to the eldest daughter, Annie, and the youngest boy, Arthur, with strict guardianship precautions for the latter. So ended Act I of Volume Three in the legal battles of Thomas Fallon.

There was, of course, lingering hostility between the disinherited children and those who inherited the earth. Carmel was involved in a new series of squabbles in other venues. It is reasonable to assume that the "grey eminence" of Soquel, Martina Castro, gave council to some of the litigants.

Doubts were even raised as to the actual death of Thomas Fallon, and the reports of the doctor in attendance and the final rites performed under the auspices of the Knight's Templar, carry many glaring inaccuracies and inconsistancies. A piece of testimony was given about the imminent departure of Fallon on a steamer bound for Panama, set to leave on the afternoon of his demise. The following years would show reports of Fallon being seen in London, Dublin, New Orleans, Denver, and assorted other locales. Nothing further was seen of the small container, the size of a ring box, and the large leather-bound package that two witnesses, including the manager of the Russ House, swore were given to the night porter for safe keeping on that last night. Extensive searches failed to produce either of these curious items.

Just as in his lovely Santa Cruz, morning fog obscures the beaches and mists gather in the dusk. It is an interesting idea to return back in your life and start anew, as Fallon wished on that last eve. St. Vrain's was a symbol to him of things past, things that one had hoped and dreamed for — at one time both a memory and an illusion.

All of the major events both local and national actually happened just this way. The people were all very, very real. Thomas Fallon spoke and wrote just as this Journal has recorded it. Perhaps there might be a question as to whether the lost leather-bound Journal actually fell from its hidden compartment early in the summer of 1978. This is quite normal. And to those skeptics I can only say that if it did not — it certainly should have.

T McE

Epilogue

WITHIN A VERY few years of the "death" and last entry in the
<u>Journal</u>, most of the central characters in the story were
removed from the scene. The "old woman," Martina Castro, died
in 1890, leaving behind a host of descendants and a conflicting legacy.
Vallejo, the fox of Sonoma, died that same year. John Charles Fremont
died penniless in Los Angeles in 1892, living on the generosity of a
railroad magnate, in a land that he had been a primary force in pro-
moting and developing. The faithful Godey had died three years
before in the Sisters Hospital of Los Angeles, with his new wife, half
a century junior, to him, by his side. Of the immediate family, Carmel
lived until 1923, a woman of extra ordinary wealth and intelligence,
whose million dollar estate was the catalyst for another bout of Court
proceedings. A final settlement of these assets, originally derived from
the King of Spain, was "amicably" arrived at between Annie, Arthur,
and four grandchildren in 1928. The two primary beneficiaries of the
parental largesse, the spritely, philanthropic actress, Ann, and the
eccentric miser, Arthur, lived well into the twentieth century. Ann can
be seen looking down from a float in one of the "Fiesta de las Rosas"
Parades, bedecked in a sign proclaiming "Daughter of Thomas Fallon;"
the float was donated by Senator James Phelan. So ends the basic
story.

Thomas Fallon is chiefly recalled by a historic marker on the
corner of Market and Post Streets in San Jose which reads:

"On this spot stood the juzgado of 1798. Over its roof Captain
Thomas Fallon raised the stars and stripes July 14, 1846."

The home which was the joy of his life and the pride of San Jose
sits in crumbling, peeling disarray. No more do the beautiful orchards
surround his mansion nor the mustard plants flow down to the Guadalupe Creek. The Sisters of Notre Dame, the Peraltas, the Pelliers are
also gone, seen only on the occasional plaque or in a footnoted reference in some work of larger scope.

So passes the glory of the world. Fallon understood this at the
end, for he belonged to that world and there is no doubt that he would
feel much less comfortable in ours.

Acknowledgements

I would like to thank the Bancroft Library, the Special Collections of the University of California at Santa Cruz, and the San Jose Historical Museum for the generous use of their photographs. The staff of the California Room at the San Jose Public Library provided much needed information, as did the ultimate resource in this section of the world, Clyde Arbuckle. I thank Mary P. Canepa for her research and criticism, and also John and Jill for their many suggestions. Pat and Terry were an invaluable help, as was the timely aid of Naomi McKay. I owe a particular debt to John Sinclair of New Brighton, who shares with me a special empathy for T. F., which I hope has resulted in some proselytism to a small degree.

List of Illustrations

PRINTING, DESIGN AND LAYOUT

BY

SMITH McKAY PRINTING COMPANY

❀   ❀   ❀

THE PAPER IS CURTIS DELMARVA TEXT

THE BOOK HAS BEEN SET IN CALEDONIA TYPEFACE
BY CASSIDAY COMPOSITION SERVICE WITH RODEO
FOR HEADINGS AND INITIAL LETTERS.

1978

SAN JOSE, CALIFORNIA